The
GUIDING
HAND

Published by

 GENERAL STORE
PUBLISHING HOUSE

Box 28, 1694B Burnstown, Ontario, Canada K0J 1G0
Telephone (613) 432-7697 or 1-800-465-6072

ISBN 1-894263-79-0
Printed and bound in Canada

Cover, layout and design by Derek McEwen
Cartoons by Dow
Printing by Custom Printers of Renfrew Ltd.

©General Store Publishing House
Burnstown, Ontario, Canada

National Library of Canada Cataloguing in Publication

Muzeen, Bernard J., 1937-
The guiding hand / Bernard J. Muzeen.

ISBN 1-894263-79-0

1. Boys and Girls Club of Ottawa-Carleton—History.
2. Muzeen, Bernard J., 1937-. I Title.

HS3260.C34B69 2003   369.4'09713'83   C2003-901934-9

DEDICATION

Dedicated with fond regards to Carol and Glenn Shortt.
Their unconditional friendship, encouragement,
approbation, faith and acceptance, in over forty years
of community and youth work, served as a bulwark
in times of challenge and triumph.

CONTENTS

PROLOGUE 7

PART I: THE BOYS AND GIRLS CLUB OF
       OTTAWA–CARLETON 9
   A Brief History of the Club 10
   The Early Days of Our Club 11
   Skateboarding Program 12
   Access for Disabled Children 16
   Special Needs Program and Services 20
   The Diefenbaker Encounters 24
   Sixty-fifth Anniversary Royal Visit 28

PART II: REAL LIFE DRAMA 31
   The Rescue of Nigel 32
   Jake's Rescue 38
   Breath of Life 40
   A Shot in the Park 44
   The Hit and Run 50

PART III: GUIDANCE & BEHAVIOUR MODIFICATION 53
   A Word to the Wise 54
   A Question of Comprehension 56
   Alternative Wording 70
   Garbage Mouth 71
   Locker Room Talk 75
   The Soap Treatment 76
   It's in the Book 79
   Promises Made/Promises Kept 82
   All for One 88
   Children Live What They Learn 92

PART IV: HUMAN INTEREST & HUMOUR 93
   Viceregal Protector . . . ? 94
   A Little Mud Won't Hurt 96
   Them's the Breaks 101
   Sensitive Situations 103

PART V: CONFLICT & RESOLUTION 111

Blood Brothers 112

They're Ripped Off 115

A Very Angry Young Man 119

There's Foam Everywhere! 125

Hand in Glove 131

A Question of Hair 139

The Colour of His Hair! 142

PART VI: BULLIES 145

Penalizing a Verbal Bully 146

Bully in the Making 150

The Avenger 152

He's My Friend 155

PART VII: CAMP MINWASSIN 159

A Royal Visit 160

Letters From Summer Camp 163

Breathe on Me . . . if You Dare! 165

Campers' Revolt 169

The Camp Mimic 173

The Butterfly Wing 175

EPILOGUE: THANK YOU FOR REMEMBERING 178

RECORD OF CHILDREN AND YOUTH SERVICES 180

PROLOGUE

The search for my family roots, suggested as a Centennial Year project by my dear friend Carol Shortt, was reluctantly undertaken by a "war orphan" who had little expectation for a positive outcome.

Armed with the vague recollections of a child in hospital and from the orphanage teachers that my family lived in Manchester and Highbury, London, before WWII, I departed for England in 1969. It became apparent that I was ill prepared. Apart from financial limitations, the lack of birth and death dates and the addresses of family members meant this undertaking was doomed.

During a sightseeing tour of London, I walked down Fleet Street towards St. Paul's Cathedral to discover the offices of *The Manchester Guardian*. On an impulse I placed the following advertisement: "Anyone knowing the Prophets of Manchester or the Muzeens of Highbury, London, please write," followed by my name and address.

Nine weeks later a letter, with "R. Muzeen" written in the upper left-hand corner, arrived. It was the first communication I had ever received from a person using my family name. Robert reported he was unaware of family members living in Canada. At his invitation, I immediately mailed to him information including: birth certificates, history of my life in orphanages, the college I attended, and newspaper clippings. After three months had passed with no response, Glenn Shortt—whose family had all but adopted me after my arrival in Canada in 1958—encouraged me to get on with life and not to linger on "what might have been."

Consequently, I happily immersed myself in working at the Boys and Girls Club of Ottawa–Carleton. It provided a professional, challenging, stimulating and rewarding experience, while meeting the unfolding needs and expectations of children and youth six to eighteen years of age.

Imagine my shock when an envelope with "R. Muzeen" written in the upper left-hand corner arrived at Christmas in 1987. Enclosed with a Christmas card was this brief note:

> My father Walter died in September. I inherited his papers and those of Robert. It seems that between when he wrote to you and your reply he became ill and died. Your letter remained unanswered for eighteen years.

One can speculate as to how my life might have changed had that 1969 letter been answered promptly. Call it providence, divine intervention, coincidence or fate that could have set in motion a chain of events resulting in my never working at the Boys and Girls Club of Ottawa–Carleton.

Had that been the case, many of the happy and challenging events in my life, some of which are told in the pages following, might never have happened.

Part I

The Boys and Girls Club of Ottawa–Carleton

A BRIEF HISTORY OF THE CLUB

In the early 1920s many families lacked a father figure in the home due to military service—and death—in Europe as the result of WWI.

During the post-war years many of these fatherless boys were getting into trouble at school and in the community at large. This resulted in repeated appearances of these wayward boys before Magistrate Glenn E. Strike (later provincial court judge) and Family Court Judge Jack McKnight. Something had to be done to provide guidance for these youths.

Consequently, after much research and planning in 1921–22, the Ottawa Boys Club opened in 1923, under the leadership of Fred C. McCann, in the St. Patrick's Literary and Scientific Association building. The program was focused on boys. However, members' sisters were permitted to attend the Boys Club on special occasions.

Thirty years later, as the Centre Town Clubhouse was being constructed, the needs of girls were raised once again. Regrettably, the building plans failed to include any basic facilities to accommodate females.

Undaunted, members of the Soroptimists Club sponsored a program for girls, one day per week, for sisters of Boys Club members, as recommended by Velma Reid in 1956. Responding with their enthusiastic participation the program for girls was expanded to three days a week by 1968. Following modest renovations in the mid-1970s, a full-time membership was open to girls. This historic step was due in great part to the leadership of Phyllis Throop, Chairman, Service Committee of the Soroptimists Club. The opening of the Fred C. McCann Clubhouse was the occasion to change the name to the Ottawa Boys and Girls Club.

Throughout the '70s and into the early '80s the national offices of the Boys Clubs of Canada, Boys Clubs of America, and the Boys Clubs of the United Kingdom monitored the effects of our Boys and Girls Club on its members and on the community.

It is a lasting tribute to the vision, challenge, accomplishments and leadership of Phyllis Throop, the Club's volunteer board of directors, service clubs, United Way, and the deep wellspring of community support, that the Ottawa concept of a boys and girls club has received worldwide acceptance.

Following construction and dedication of the Britannia Clubhouse in 1981, our organization changed its name to The Boys and Girls Club of Ottawa–Carleton. It reflects the reality that thousands of children and youth living in the communities adjacent to Ottawa consider the Boys and Girls Club as "their home away from home."

It has been estimated that the lives of more than 250,000 children and youth have been enriched as a result of the day-to-day social, physical, educational, cultural, recreational and guidance services provided by the Boys and Girls Club of Ottawa–Carleton since it was founded in 1923 by Fred C. McCann.

A "snow war" with members of the Britannia Clubhouse. This feature was a regular highlight of our midwinter festival and was introduced following the dedication of the Britannia Clubhouse in 1981.   *Courtesy of* The Ottawa Citizen

THE EARLY DAYS OF OUR CLUB

Through the determination and the sheer willpower of Fred McCann, our Boys Club survived many a crisis during its formative years and in the ensuing five decades while it was under his leadership.

Gordon Henderson, QC, a founding member of the Boys Club, recalls his first childhood encounter with Fred McCann in 1923: "I remember that day when the two O'Connor boys, Kincaid and myself were playing a game of 'Kip-on-the-Run' in the Cartier Square Park. A man came up and asked if we would be interested in joining an organized club."

That man was of course Fred C. McCann, the founding executive director of the Ottawa Boys Club, as it was then known.

"Fiesher, Miller, Kincaid, Marion, Juneau, O'Connor and Riopell are some of the family names I can recall from those early boyhood days at the Club. We had some pretty rough characters from Centre Town and Sandy Hill. But the counselling and guidance they received at the Club helped bring order to their lives," Gordon Henderson recalled during a 1979 interview for the *Clubhouse News*.

"One of my most vivid memories of those early days at the Club was a fire at the armouries. It caused small arms to explode with spectacular results. Another thing I remember is that in those days plus-fours, shirts and ties were the dress of the day," Henderson recalled as he looked through photographs in the Club archives.

"The advantage of the Ottawa Boys Club was that it offered facilities, organization and encouragement for so many of us. Hockey, basketball, ping-pong, boxing, baseball and—oh yes, basket weaving—were popular," he added with a smile.

Gordon Henderson was among the first four boys to join the organization in 1923. He served as an advisory board member of the Ottawa Boys and Girls Club some forty years later. "I have a clear recollection of organized groups and teams such as St. Bridget's Parish, The Shamrocks, The Gunner's Club, Rideau Aquatic Club, the YMCA and the Boys Club," he continued. "We sported crests on our jackets as a manifestation of our accomplishments gained under the direction of men such as Mr. Cheveiere, a Lisgar teacher, with chums such as Andy Gratton, 'Mus' Burns, Emil Desgenais and Rick Perley."

In the intervening eighty years the organization, now the Boys and Girls Club of Ottawa, is estimated to have extended a guiding hand to more than 250,000 members from six to eighteen years of age.

This remarkable accomplishment is due in great part to the ongoing commitment of thousands of dedicated volunteers and supportive donors who envision our Boys and Girls Club to be a positive investment in our community's most precious resource for the future, **children and youth**.

Our Boys and Girls Club continues to fulfill the hopes, aspirations, expectations and foresight of Fred C. McCann, and the dedicated band of concerned citizens who seek to make a difference for good in the lives of our young people.

SKATEBOARDING PROGRAM

In the early seventies the City of Ottawa undertook to discourage skateboarding on its sidewalks, streets, facilities and parking properties. The rapid—some would say overnight—increase of participants in this highly popular youth-oriented sport caught both the elected and appointed officials by surprise.

Banning skateboarding, which many saw as just another fad, received wide approval from the adult population as a wise and reasoned measure. However, young people felt that it was a form of collective punishment and discrimination.

In community discussion groups young people pointed out that their local taxes go to provide facilities and subsidies to adult-oriented sports such as lawn bowling, golf, and curling. However, the city's recreation department could not—or would not—fund a location for this popular youth sporting activity.

Youngsters pointed out that they pay taxes on the wide array of equipment they use. Others pointed out that the very stores that sell skateboard equipment pay a license fee to the City of Ottawa. Young people felt that the action of the local government sent the unquestionable message that youth don't count when their needs are seen to clash with those of adults.

Consequently, local malls, federal property, bike paths, school facilities, NCC locations, church lots, and even the National War Memorial in Confederation Square, were inundated by skateboarders given nowhere else to enjoy their growing sport.

In the late spring of the year that the "anti-skateboarding by-law" was being enforced, Scott Howarth visited me in the Centre Town Clubhouse of the Boys and Girls Club of Ottawa–Carleton.

"You wouldn't let us skateboard in here, would you?" he asked.

"Scott, are you telling me something I should know or asking me a question?"

"It's a question. Can we skateboard in here? Please!" was his firm response.

"Is this for only you or have you got a number of friends who would be interested in skateboarding?"

"Lots of guys. Really lots of 'em!"

"And what about safety equipment rules?"

"Do we have to?" Scott asked.

I nodded my head affirmatively.

"Elbow and knee pads. Right?" Scott stated.

"Don't forget the helmet. Wear elbow pads, kneepads and helmets, at all times. Otherwise no skateboarding."

"All right," rolling his eyes.

"You must all take out a Club membership, without exceptions," I stated firmly.

"Sounds fair to me. When can we start?" was his next question.

Referring to the program schedule for the gymnasium, I discovered that there were two open periods as a result of the conclusion of the Ball Hockey League games.

"How about 7:00 p.m. to 9:00 p.m. on Tuesdays and Thursdays for the last two weeks of April and all of May? They're now available."

"Wow! That's great!" He shook my hand.

"You're welcome, Scott."

"When can I start?"

"This evening if you wish."

"I'll be here."

"Scott, I thought you said there would be lots of skate-boarders. You do understand I can't justify designating a whole program period for just one or two riders."

"How many should . . . er . . . be enough, Bernie?"

"No less than fifteen. But mind you, all with safety gear. Okay?"

"That's fair!" Scott exclaimed.

"That should tell us if there is sufficient interest to include skateboarding in our Club schedule for the fall season," I explained.

After Scott had departed I headed for the coordinator of physical education to share the good news. He showed little or no enthusiasm at the prospect of skateboarding as part of his program schedule. Furthermore, his hands were filled each Tuesday and Thursday evening with a very active baseball

Brent Jordan, Boys and Girls Club skateboard champion. In the early '70s he assisted in the design and construction of a "half-pipe" in the Centre Town Clubhouse.
Courtesy of The Ottawa Citizen

league, in the Centennial School field across the street from our clubhouse.

Thus it fell to me to supervise the skateboard program.

It proved to be a happy association with hundreds of enthusiastic young athletes for almost twenty years at our club.

During the first ten of my retirement years I was beseeched by skateboarders in the city of Kanata and the village of Stittsville to serve as their instructor. So many youngsters expressed a never-ending wonderment that someone as old as I knew so much about this sport; nevertheless they were eager to be taught by me. It was a joyful endeavour that continues up to the date of writing this series of recollections.

Skateboarding highlights over those years include:
- Design, construction, and funding of ramps and rail slides by the skateboarders in a basement room known as "The Dustbowl."
- Active participation by Jim Minty, who became Canadian's first skateboard champion.

- Canada Day feature acts on Parliament Hill and Major Hill's Park site for four years.
- Demonstrations for Rideau Hall; the United Way Campaigns; local elementary schools; and corporate and community picnics.
- Summer skateboarding facilities being made available in Kanata, Gloucester, and Stittsville.
- A thrilling demonstration of skateboarding for TRH the Duke and Duchess of York during the sixty-fifth anniversary year celebrations of the Boys and Girls Club of Ottawa–Carleton.
- The conversion of the Stittsville Hockey Arena into a full service skateboard park for the summer season, which attracted hundreds of skateboarders and rollerbladers from far and wide. (Stittsville, which has the largest per capita youth population in the Ottawa–Carleton Region, had offered very limited recreational social activities for its young residents.)
- Involvement by royalty when HRH Prince Andrew stopped his limousine to ask skateboarders to show some respect for the Canadian National War Memorial, in Confederation Square, by refraining from riding on it.

The author installs the sixty-fifth anniversary year logo at the front door of the Centre Town Clubhouse, in the spring of 1988.   *Courtesy of* The Ottawa Citizen

ACCESS FOR DISABLED CHILDREN

Between 1971 and 1989, the number of physically and emotionally challenged children and youth that integrated into the day-to-day, year-round activities and services of the Boys and Girls Club of Ottawa–Carleton grew from eight to well over 320.

The genesis of the program can be traced to a sunny day in May 1971. Arriving at the Centre Town Clubhouse, I encountered a fourteen-year-old in a motorized wheelchair at the foot of the four concrete steps that led up to the front door.

"Hi!" the young man greeted me.

"Hello. My name is Bernie." I responded, extending my right hand. Immediately I realized that my visitor was not able to extend his right hand in greeting.

"Hello. My name is Brian," he said, waving his right hand slightly, while resting his wrist on the arm of his wheelchair. "What do you guys do in there?"

"We offer all kinds of fun activities such as pool, snooker, and table tennis. We have a library, craft shop, weight room, gymnasium, swimming pool, a kitchen and a darkroom." I paused.

"We have a swimming pool too," the boy stated.

"Where?"

"Over there. In Centennial School." He inclined his head to indicate its direction.

"Oh. I should try to get over to see it. Who should I ask?"

"Mrs. Gray. She can arrange that!"

"Thanks, Brian," I added as I walked up the steps to the front door.

"I guess I'll never get in there to see that place," he commented more to himself than to me.

"Why not? Can you hold on for a moment, Brian?" I asked while placing my hand on the door handle.

"Sure." He said, as he turned a complete circle in his wheelchair.

Returning with the custodian and maintenance man, the three of us carefully lifted Brian and his motorized wheelchair up the four concrete steps. Once inside, he wheeled his way through the gym and the locker room, to the observation window at the pool, and finally into a junior members games room, all of which are located on the main floor of the building.

"Wow!" was his delighted expression at each new discovery.

"The weight room and that other stuff . . . ?" his voice trailed off.

"Oh. They are on the second floor and in the basement," I said.

"I've got to go," Brian said abruptly as he glanced at the clock and realized it was nearly 1:00 p.m.

"How come?"

"I'll be late getting back to school."

"Don't worry. I will come over to Centennial School with you and explain to the teacher why you are late."

The Centre Town Clubhouse, which was constructed in the mid-fifties, had no elevator, limiting access to two-thirds of the building for wheelchair-bound individuals.

"Thank you, sir," he smiled as the three of us placed him gently on the sidewalk.

"Hey . . . My name is Bernie."

There was quite an excited commotion in the corridor of the school as Brian relayed the details of his visit to the Boys and Girls Club.

"They will all want to go over now," Mrs. Gray advised, with a knowing look on her face. Several dozen students in wheelchairs, and some using crutches and walking frames surrounded us.

"I had better talk to the principal," I said.

"Mmmm . . . " was her response.

So it was arranged, following a conversation with the Centennial School principal, that Brian's fellow students could visit the clubhouse in groups of four, during the noon hour, over the next ten school days.

In a remarkable show of willpower and courage the more ambulatory youngsters determinedly tackled the stairs to explore the basement and second floor of the clubhouse, followed by volunteers carrying their crutches and walking frames.

Given the repeated requests from these children, their teachers and parents, our clubhouse undertook to explore the feasibility of providing a series of activities during the lunch hour, two days a week commencing in the fall of 1971.

Guidelines were developed:

- The activities would be typical of those offered other Club members.
- These activities would be adapted to facilitate the specific limitations of the participants.
- All participants would take out Club memberships.
- In the event of rain or snow the program would be moved to the Centennial School.
- One volunteer would be required for each wheelchair-bound youngster. Students of Immaculata High School, west of the clubhouse, happily volunteered to participate in this program.

In an effort to avoid the "disabled" label, these youngsters were invited to assist in developing a name. During a brainstorming session one student, Kevin I think it was, pointed out that Mrs. Gray's classroom and their physical treatments took place in the south wing of their school. Consequently, their program became the South Wingers Club and the youngsters took pride in being known as "South Wingers."

"There is a place for able and disabled children together in our Boys and Girls Club," declared the board of directors. The growth and success of the Special Needs Program provided years of joy, acceptance, leadership, personal growth, fulfillment and enrichment for thousands of youngsters, their parents, and our community.

These unsolicited comments were received as the program expanded to our three clubhouses:

> We are pleased that the Boys and Girls Club is once again providing activities for Special Needs students of our school. This is the fourteenth consecutive year in which Centennial students have benefited from the care and concern of the staff and volunteers of your Centre Town Clubhouse.   *James E. Williamson, Principal*

> I would like to comment on how this type of programme (Special Needs) not only benefits Mike, but also all the other children who are involved in the Centre Town Clubhouse.
>
> Because Mike is quite noticeably "different" in some ways, people— children and adults—perceive him as "handicapped" and mentally write him off as being deficient in all ways. However, given Mike's strength, your "normal" children are constantly amazed when he is far above them in capability in doing such things as model-making and the like.
>
> I believe that this type of experience is enriching and certainly gives them a different perspective in dealing with any handicapped person in the future.   *Judi Roy, Parent*

> A major goal for our mentally/physically handicapped students is to learn to live in their community and to become accepted citizens. Learning recreational, social, interpersonal skills are crucial to achieving this goal. The weekly classroom visits have extended into the students' evening and weekend life. Parents of handicapped children now have a community resource available to them.
>
> There are very few community recreational facilities available for handicapped adolescents, unlike the number available for the non-handicapped children.   *Heather Crowe, Special Education*

> My name is Shelly Dumulong. I have been a member for two years at the Boys & Girls Club of Ottawa–Carleton.
>
> I like going to the Centre Town Clubhouse because it's lots of fun. When I go to the Club I play games; take the Babysitting Course; play in the gym; and in the swimming pool. I am in the "red level." In the summer I went to a Penny Carnival, and did an "Air Band" with my sister. I went to the McCann Clubhouse for "Awareness Day," where I

enjoyed watching Dean Melway's demonstration. The thing I like best about the people with special needs is that they are my friends.

Shelly Dumulong, Club Member

We are most grateful to you and to the members of the Ottawa Boys and Girls Club for the wonderful facilities available to handicapped children. As you know our son Stephen attended the Centre Town Unit from 1975 until 1980, when we lived in the Glebe area.

Since our move to the west end of the city, our son has participated in activities for the handicapped at your Britannia Unit. We have noticed over the years that Stephen has greatly benefited from the programs you offer, the understanding and expertise of your staff, and the comradeship he enjoys with other handicapped youngsters. It has indeed helped him to develop his potential to the fullest.

Stephen always looked forward to his visits to the Boys and Girls Club and needless to say, it helps the morale of our family as well to see the enjoyment he derived from your programs.

Mrs. Ralph Sisson, Parent

On the eve of the eightieth anniversary year of our Boys and Girls Club it's heartening to learn that the "integration activities" continue to be accessible to all children and youth, regardless of ability, thanks to the co-operation of prime support agencies, community volunteers, and the United Way, plus designated financial gifts from caring donors.

Apple dunking, one of the many special events enjoyed each year at the Boys and Girls Club. This photograph was taken in the mid-seventies to assist in promoting the United Way Campaign.   *Andrews Newton*

A personal observation: My empathy and passion for the inclusion of the physically disabled stems from my own childhood experiences.

As a young child I was stricken with osteomyelitis. It required many operations; hospitalization; a wheelchair-bound childhood; leg braces during my teenage years; and ongoing discomfort throughout my adult life.

Often students mockingly referred to me as "the poor wee cripple" at school.

I was excluded from many school activities. With the passage of time I learned to exploit my disability when distinguished guests visited our orphanage. I fondly recall the visit of Johnny Leach, the British table tennis champion. I had deftly manoeuvred my wheelchair to the front row. After he prevented a student from removing me to the back row, Johnny selected me to play a demonstration table tennis game . . .

At twelve years of age I resolved never to allow anyone to exclude me—or others—from fully participating in life because of a physical disability.

SPECIAL NEEDS PROGRAMS AND SERVICES

Objectives:

1. To facilitate the integration of children and youth with special needs into the day-to-day activities of the Club.

2. To heighten the awareness among able-bodied Club members of the abilities of those with special needs.

3. To facilitate the participation of those with special needs into the community mainstream.

4. To provide training opportunities for companions/friends to those with special needs.

5. To truly make the Club accessible to **all** children and youth in keeping with our goals and objectives.

The undoubted success of the Special Needs Program and Services of the Boys and Girls Club of Ottawa–Carleton, which commenced in 1971, is clearly due to the wellspring of community support and goodwill that has been built up since 1923.

Countless individuals, groups and organizations throughout Ottawa–Carleton opened their hearts, arms and schedules to ensure the success of this humanitarian and noble undertaking.

Some highlights, program participants and sources of valuable assistance:

- Lorie Corkery, Lynn Upton, Barbara Zarzycky and Colleen Higginson were awarded the Ontario Medal for Good Citizenship for their personal and collective leadership in coordinating Immaculata High School students who volunteered to serve as companion/friend to special needs students from Centennial School. Lorie, Lynn, Barbara and Colleen were the first teenagers ever to receive this prestigious award for volunteer community service from the government of Ontario.

- The Ottawa 67's hockey team happily participated in vigorous games of "sit down hockey." The South Wingers delighted in scoring goals and having their guests penalized for "raising their butts" from their chairs. These sporting encounters became treasured moments in their young lives.

- Visits by Ottawa Rough Rider football players proved to be a wonderful thrill for star-struck football fans. The Rough Riders would toss the football and share ball-handling techniques. Many South Wingers updated the personal static record of their favourite player

- Students from Ashbury College made valuable contributions that facilitated the integration of disabled children and youth into the "After Four" activities, by serving as companion/friend, in our Centre Town Clubhouse.

- The Rotary Club of Ottawa underwrote the construction of the access ramp from the sidewalk to the clubhouse front door. Rotarians also provided financial assistance that enabled the Club to secure the services of specially trained part-time staff as the registration of physically and emotionally challenged members grew annually.

- The Children's Hospital of Eastern Ontario, special education teachers, children at risk, parents of disabled children, and social service agencies, among others, found the development of leisure time activities and recreational and social interaction skills in the informal setting of our Club to ". . . have been very helpful in formulating programs to try and integrate these children with their normal peers . . ."

- Thanks to "designated gifts," an elevator was installed in order to make the Centre Town Clubhouse fully accessible to wheelchair-bound members and volunteers.

- The Fred C. McCann and Britannia clubhouses were designed and constructed barrier-free, thanks to the generosity of building fund donors.

- Summer Works grants from the federal government enabled our three clubhouses to offer a series of "awareness programs" for non-handicapped youngsters.

- The Ken Spratt Memorial Hockey Game, chaired by Sgt. Douglas Kirkland and sponsored by the Ottawa Police Association, generated revenue to sustain the Special Needs Program over many years.

- Brian Smith, sports reporter with CJOH TV, a Club alumnus and a keen supporter of the Special Needs Program, was a frequent and popular visitor. Brian gave generously of his time and talents, which ensured the success of many community projects for the Club.

- Provincial Court Judge Bernard Ryan provided South Wingers with an opportunity to learn about the function of the courts. In a mock trial, Bernie, "who forgot to bring the weekly treat," was found guilty and ordered "to double the weekly treat next session." While this wise judgment was greeted with sustained cheering, the South Wingers did learn that what really happens in a court of law is a far cry from what is portrayed in most television shows.

- Thanks to the generosity of donors, buildings in Camp Minwassin are now wheelchair accessible.

- Scores of volunteers established a one-on-one buddy system that enabled the increasing number of physically challenged youngsters to enjoy access to the "super-heated swimming pool" in Centennial School. This extension of Centre Town Clubhouse's evening program, started in the mid-eighties, proved to be very popular.

* * *

Here is some unsolicited correspondence that reflects the feelings of the community:

I have a six-year-old boy who has a genetic skin condition called lamellar ichthyosis.

Frankly I was quite anxious about Mikey using the Club on McArthur Street this summer. However, because I work close by I decided to try leaving Mikey at the Club with his brother and sister. I was quite delighted and amazed at how well Mikey was integrated into the mainstream of Club activities.

The special needs coordinator was able to assure me that the few specific needs unique to Mikey's condition could easily be accommodated. He also seemed to serve as a guardian angel helping both Mikey and others at the Club to understand and accept one another.   *Stephen Shanahan, Parent*

Your co-operation in providing us with needed recreational facilities, the gymnasium and swimming pool (for in-patients of the psychiatric unit of the Children's Hospital) is much appreciated. However, beyond this, your organization does at this point represent an integral aspect of our therapeutic strategy both through providing a normalizing activity oriented setting, by means of which we can effectively maintain our children in the community, and by providing support and follow-up for the children who return home.

Many of these youngsters especially lack confidence with peers and rely on the informal supervision you provide. Your skill in facilitating this delicate process is much appreciated.

H.H. Popham, President, C.H.E.O. Foundation

I would like to let you know how I feel about the learning delayed children in the Club. It is nice to see your staff work with these children in the Club.

It will let the other children help and understand learning delayed children. They have been kept away long enough from regular children. It is very nice to see that someone really cares about these children.

Florence Deacon, Parent

Our organization, the Communication Development Program of Children at Risk, deals primarily with autistic and communication disordered children. Our children often have difficulty in social interaction and developing recreational skills.

The special needs coordinators, at all three of your units, have been very helpful in formulating programs to try to integrate these children with their normal peers. We have found them to be extremely supportive and very understanding of the needs of autistic and communication disordered individuals.

Their work has been greatly appreciated and the programs now in place provide the opportunity for the children to develop social and recreational skills. We hope to continue our present involvement with your program and feel that the role played by the special needs coordinators is important.   *J.L. Stadnyk, Director, Children at Risk*

The reason for this letter is to express our hope that the Special Needs Program will continue into the New Year.

Our staff feel that the special needs coordinator, Mr. Ted Ross, is extremely competent and sensitive to the needs of our students.

The students attending our school have emotional problems and some behavioural problems as a result. Several students have expressed an interest in attending your Club after school hours; the majority would have never heard of the Club without the opportunity we presented to them under the direction of Mr. Ross.

We feel that your Club provides not only the guidance and support these students need, but also a perfect chance for appropriate social interaction.   *Bonnie L. Radmore, Teacher, M.F. McHugh School*

On the eve of the eightieth anniversary year of the Boys and Girls Club, it's heartening to know that the Special Needs Programs and Services continue to be accessible to all children and youth.

Commentary:

- Our Boys and Girls Club nominated Lorie Corkery, Lynn Upton, Barbara Zarzycky and Colleen Higginson for the Ontario Medal for Good Citizenship in 1974.

- Officials of the Ontario government requested that only one of the four teenagers be designated as "the most deserving individual, as this award cannot be presented to groups."

- We are advised that it took the personal intervention of Premier Bill Davis to ensure that this wonderful example of volunteer service and good citizenship, by each of these teenagers, would be honoured.

- It's ironic that after years of volunteer service with disabled children, Lorie would one day be disabled as a result of an accident.

- "She now understands the frustration of the Centennial students when she and her able-bodied friends tried to do things *for* them. Now that she's disabled, like those Centennial School students, Lorie is determined to do as much as she can for herself," said Mrs. Corkery.

THE DIEFENBAKER ENCOUNTERS

The Rt. Hon. John George Diefenbaker, former prime minister of Canada, has had a number of heartfelt and touching experiences with members of the Boys and Girls Club of Ottawa–Carleton.

In his capacity as dean of the House of Commons, this Right Honourable gentleman showed a keen interest in the local and national activities of the Boys and Girls Club movement. These ranged from a U.S.A. Bicentennial Ceremony; presentation of *The Convention on the Rights of the Child* to the House of Commons by a delegation of Club members from across Canada during the International Year of the Child; the dedication of the Heritage Room of the Boys and Girls Club of Ottawa–Carleton; plus being the guest of honour during the fifty-fifth anniversary celebration of Camp Minwassin.

The following are brief descriptions of those "Diefenbaker Experiences" with Club members.

Bicentennial

The Congress of the United States designated our Boys and Girls Club, the only non-American organization to be so honoured, as an official celebration site for the Bicentennial of the United States. The Rt. Hon. John G. Diefenbaker joined Bruce Middleton, Boy of the Year; William Robinson, president of the board of directors; and R.M. Wood and myself in accepting from the American ambassador a Congressional Citation and the bicentennial flag. The presentation took place at the Canadian Centennial flame on Parliament Hill.

Rights of the Child

The United Nations declared 1979 the International Year of the Child, while reaffirming its 1959 *Declaration of the Rights of the Child*. The Boys and Girls Club's national office wished to arrange a presentation of *The Convention on the Rights of the Child* to the Parliament of Canada. The Speaker of The Commons was not available to receive the delegation of Club members from each of the provinces and territories. That duty was happily accepted by Mr. Diefenbaker, in his capacity as dean of the House of Commons.

Accepting copies of *The Convention on the Rights of the Child* in both official languages, he undertook to bring this important document to the attention of all the Members of Parliament on behalf of all the children of Canada. The former prime minister took this occasion to chat with each of the young delegates. His recollections of visiting the hometowns of a number of these youngsters provided a personal and heartfelt interaction that would resonate with each individual for many years.

Heritage Room

To celebrate in 1973 the fiftieth anniversary year of the founding of the Ottawa Boys Club (as it was then), the Centre Town Clubhouse Junior Leaders Corps, co-chaired by Steven Martin and Gordon Johnson, created the Heritage Room to display Club crests, trophies, old newspaper clippings, photographs, handwritten minutes of 1923 board meetings, and 8-mm home movies by Fred C. McCann, plus many of the national and international awards bestowed upon the club founder.

The junior leaders extended an invitation to Mr. Diefenbaker to open their Heritage Room. After the opening ceremonies he graciously shared with 150 Club members a story from his boyhood:

> Accompanied by my mother and brother, we took a train trip to Prince Albert, Saskatchewan, to join my father. Now in those days, trains did not have upholstered seats. You sat on hard wooden benches. Not very comfortable, you know.

> A most remarkable sight on this long train trip, during those very hot summer days, were the mounds of white snow every twenty miles or so, as we crossed the prairies. You can understand how much my brother and I dearly wanted the train to stop, if only to give us a chance to enjoy a cool, refreshing treat.

Hundreds of alumni and friends fill Salons A, B, and C at Lansdowne Park in Ottawa for the fiftieth anniversary year dinner and celebration of the Ottawa Boys Club In 1973.
Canadian Press

Finally, that opportunity occurred. Without telling our mother, my brother and I got off that train and ran as fast as our legs would go, on that very hot summer day, towards our prize . . . those glistening mounds of snow!

You can imagine how devastated we were when all those mounds proved to be the sun-bleached bones of the thousands of buffalo killed by pioneers. Farmers had to collect up all these bones before their ploughs could cut the soil. This area is presently renowned for its fields of golden wheat. So the next time you see something from afar, be careful—it may not be what you expect.

Mr. Diefenbaker participated in a forty-five-minute question and answer period with members. This was followed by a slice of the fiftieth anniversary cake and a soft drink for everyone. Too bad there was no ice cream!

Camp Anniversary

In the summer of 1978 Mr. Diefenbaker was the guest of honour at the fifty-fifth Anniversary Day celebrations of Camp Minwassin, on the shores of Mink

The Right Honourable John G. Diefenbaker, the former prime minister of Canada, enjoys an ice cream treat during the fifty-fifth anniversary year celebrations at Camp Minwassin.   *Courtesy of* The Ottawa Citizen

Lake, near Eganville. Following demonstrations of camping skills, watercraft, and pioneering ability on that very hot summer day, our guest of honour decreed that ice cream had to be served to everyone—no doubt a recollection of his childhood desire for this particular refreshing treat!

SIXTY-FIFTH ANNIVERSARY YEAR ROYAL VISIT

In July 1989 Their Royal Highnesses The Duke and Duchess of York joined members, friends, supporters, and community leaders in celebrating the sixty-fifth anniversary of the founding of our Boys and Girls Club.

A portion of my report to the board of directors of the Club stated:

> It was a real life experience that the royal couple lingered well past their scheduled departure time; one can only conclude that the feeling was mutual. The excited recollections of Club members, in the months following this royal visit, confirm that their memories of this gracious couple, who showed a genuine interest in each youngster, will last a lifetime.

Prince Andrew learns all about skateboarding from members of the highly skilled team that provided a thrilling show during our sixty-fifth anniversary year celebration.
Government of Canada

Their Royal Highnesses the Duke and Duchess of York are greeted upon their arrival for the sixty-fifth anniversary year festival, held in the Centre Town Clubhouse.

Government of Canada

PART II

Real Life Drama

THE RESCUE OF NIGEL

Note: Only the name of the central character has been changed for his protection. All other names are real.

I was busy in my office trying to catch up with the backlog of paperwork necessary for the smooth operation of our Boys and Girls Club. I became aware of a hubbub from the front hall. A quick look at my watch confirmed that it was the supper hour.

The level of the noise from the outside of my office was more intense than usual. So I started to pay attention to what was being said.

"Why don't you go in there and tell him?" Harry, a thirty-three-year veteran worker with the Club, said in his gruff manner.

"But he's got Nigel," a child's voice explained urgently.

"Get in there and tell him!" Harry commanded.

"What's going on out there?" I called from my desk.

A moment later, Barry, accompanied by about eight or ten friends, pushed his way into my office.

"He's got Nigel. Bernie, he's got Nigel," Barry said with an even, firm tone to his voice.

"Who's got Nigel?"

"The driver of the truck. He grabbed Nigel and took off," Barry explained, an intense expression on his face.

It was clear from the agitation of the other children that something serious had occurred. Barry maintained his composure, while those who accompanied him showed their distress.

I invited Barry to be seated. Two of the boys who accompanied him insisted on remaining standing. All of the other excited youngsters were required to wait outside the open office door.

"Tell me what happened, Barry," I asked, as calmly as possible.

"The guys and I were sliding down that hill of snow, outside Centennial School. Over there on Gloucester Street," he pointed out of the window. "This green truck came by. It stopped and the man driving the truck told us he would give us money if we could beat him in a race up the hill. Only little Nigel took up his offer. The rest of us, we just continued to slide . . ." his voice trailed off.

"And?" I prompted.

"Nigel, well he ran up Gloucester Street towards Percy Street. When he got there, instead of giving him the money the guy opened the truck door and pulled Nigel in. Then the truck took off," Barry explained.

Picking up a pen, I asked the thirteen-year-old observer, "What colour was the truck?"

"It was green. A green truck, with gold lettering on its doors." His two companions nodded their heads in agreement.

"What was the license number?"

The boys looked at each other. They returned a "We don't know" shrug of their shoulders.

"Then what was the name of the company, Barry?"

"Something Gardening and Landscaping. Eh, fellows?" he said more to his friends than to me. They agreed.

"It also had one of those homemade units on the back . . . you know . . . the type that goes behind the cab. It was a grey colour, with small orange plastic windows in the side," Barry reported.

He looked to his companions, and they did not dispute his description.

My note-taking was interrupted when one of the boys asked me the very question that was racing through my mind.

"What are you going to do, Bernie?"

"I need a few more points before I call the police," I assured him. I asked, "Which direction did the truck go? What did the driver look like? What was Nigel wearing? You know, all that kind of stuff," I explained.

Before any further answers could be given, Mike, the games room supervisor, who had just returned from his supper break, entered the crowded lobby of the clubhouse.

"What's going on here? Let's clear the hall," he told the youngsters outside my office door.

"They got Nigel . . ."

"A guy kidnapped Nigel . . ."

"A truck took off with him . . ." a number of excited children informed Mike, all at once.

"What do you mean?" he said, as he pushed his way through them towards the opened door of my office.

"Are they serious?" he asked me quizzically as he cocked his head in the direction of the children in the hallway.

"Sure. Tell him, Barry," I directed.

"Mike, it was a green truck, with gold letters for a garden and landscaping company on the doors, and one of those low units on its back. Well this guy took off with Nigel," Barry restated, in his calm and steady manner.

"Get serious, Barry!" snapped Mike, as he cut the boy off in mid-sentence. "I just passed a truck like that. It's parked on Percy Street."

"Where?" everyone shouted simultaneously.

"Where did you see it, Mike?" I cut in.

"Just down the street. It's outside the Rideau Curling Rink."

"Are you sure?" Barry and I asked in unison.

"Of course!" he almost shouted, as he turned to leave the office.

The youngsters in the front hall moved en masse for the front door, to see for themselves.

A shrill blast of my ever-present whistle brought everyone to a halt in mid-stride. "Hold it!" I instructed. "Everyone remain in the clubhouse, except for

Mike and Fern. They will come with me. Is that understood?" I said firmly, to a sea of upturned faces.

An uneasy calm returned to the youngsters.

"Barry, you had better come with us to the corner of Percy and Nepean Street and tell us if it's the same truck."

"Please," I turned to the club members, "the rest of you guys stay here?"

Barry, Mike, and Fern, who is a senior club member, accompanied me to the street corner.

"That's it. That's it, Bernie," Barry said excitedly, in a hoarse whisper, as he pointed down Percy Street to where a truck stood.

I patted him on the shoulder. "Stay here, Barry. Mike, you and Fern follow me. Let's spread out, just in case," I advised as I headed south on the east sidewalk of Percy Street. I kept my eyes fixed on the truck.

It was a strange sight. There was the truck sitting on the west side of Percy Street under a bright street light. Its engine was running and the lights were on. It was enveloped in a cloud of its own exhaust, not too far from the front door of the prestigious Rideau Curling Club.

I soon came parallel with the truck cab. Looking across Percy Street, I could see the wall of the curling rink unobstructed through the truck windows.

The cab was empty.

"Damn it, it's cold," I said to myself. The cold chill of the winter night now had my full attention. I was dressed in a cotton shirt and slacks. I just wanted to get warm.

"Nothing," I shouted to Mike and Fern who were half a block behind me. "Nothing here," I called against the wind, with my hands cupped to my mouth.

Heading back to the clubhouse, somewhat annoyed that I had been taken in by Barry and his friends, I heard it. I stopped to listen . . . but only silence. It must have been the wind in the overhead wires . . . or my imagination playing tricks.

Again I proceeded to the clubhouse.

Then I heard it again. Louder this time. A quick glance at the truck window yielded only the concrete wall of the building behind it.

What I heard was a high-pitched, muffled scream. It must be coming from behind the truck or maybe from that unit on its back, or from one of the nearby houses.

Mike and Fern had by now turned back toward the clubhouse. Not wishing to alert the attacker as to my close proximity, I chose not to hail them to return.

Crossing Percy Street, I looked in the truck's cab and observed just a pile of clothing on the seat. Walking quietly to the rear unit, I peered through one of the orange plastic slit windows. Nothing, other than a few scraps of wood.

As I walked around the front of the truck, I glanced once more into the truck cab.

I noticed that the pile of clothes was moving, just slightly. I took a second look. The pile of clothes moved again.

Ever polite, I knocked on the driver's door before pulling it open.

Up sat a man.

He was dressed in dark clothing. A dark toque on his head had a narrow yellow band. I could not help but notice that the left eye danced in his head while the right eye remained still and hypnotic.

"What do you want?" he growled.

"You have my boy in there," I shouted, grabbing his shoulder with my right hand and his wrist with my left hand. I tried to climb into the cab. His right hand came out of nowhere and pushed my head back. I tightened my grip and tried not to fall backwards on the ice-slicked street.

Up popped Nigel from behind the driver.

The look on the little boys face was that of sheer terror . . . eyes wide open . . . face ashen . . . mouth ajar . . . clothes in disarray. He did not make a sound.

"That's my boy," I shouted, not taking my eyes from Nigel. I redoubled my efforts to climb into the truck.

This effort was stopped abruptly, when the driver, whom I was not watching, smashed his right fist into my face just below my left eye. The impact sent me backwards, however I refused to loosen my grip on the driver's left arm.

"Mike! Mike!" I yelled to my companions, who were last seen heading for the clubhouse. "He's here. Nigel's here," I screamed, against the wind, at the top of my lungs.

With his right hand Nigel's abductor threw the truck into gear, while his left hand held the steering wheel.

Given that the truck was sitting on a sheet of ice it moved very slowly. Still, I concentrated my efforts on pulling at the left wrist and shoulder of the driver.

The truck gained traction and lurched forward. At the same instant, I felt a searing pain in my left elbow as the opened door of the truck swung shut.

The impact on my elbow made my left hand release the driver's wrist. I still managed to hold on to his shoulder with my right hand, my back was now against the vehicle. As the truck gained traction the door was swinging against my chest and stomach. My left arm hung limply at my side.

The buffeting of the door and increasing speed of the truck forced the release of my grip on the driver's shoulder. As I turned to get out of the way of the rear wheels of the truck, I twisted my left ankle.

At that very moment, I caught one last glimpse of Nigel's anxious face. The truck pulled away from me, as it headed south, in the direction of Somerset Street.

"Get him, Mike. Get him, when he has to stop at Somerset," I shouted as he and Fern ran past me, after the truck. Given the pain in my leg, I limited my advance to the intersection of Cooper Street.

With traffic heavy on Somerset, I figured that Mike and Fern had another chance to get young Nigel out of that vehicle before it was too late.

Brake lights flashed on and off repeatedly as the truck driver forced his way into the stream of traffic, on Somerset Street. With a feeling of dread and despair, I watched the truck turn west and pass out of sight.

"I could have got him if I'd tried harder," I said to myself as I turned towards the clubhouse, dejectedly. "Should have called the police. Damn it!" I thought.

The ice-cold wind cut through me like a knife.

"He's here! Bernie, he's here!" I heard Mike yelling from behind me.

It was too much for me to hope, but it was true. Young Nigel had had the presence of mind to slip out of the truck as his captor was preoccupied with threading the vehicle through stop and start traffic, at the intersection.

Turning, I could see nothing because of the deep shadow cast by the laundromat that stood on the corner.

"He's here! Nigel's here," Mike yelled again, from the shadow of the building.

"Bring him over here. Please," I called.

Mike scooped Nigel off his feet and started to carry him towards where I stood, in the middle of Percy Street.

As Mike headed towards me, Nigel stiffened himself like a board. The little boy started to scream and scream at the top of his voice. The more Mike tried to assure him he was okay, the louder the child screamed.

"Put him down. Let him walk," I shouted. "Put him down," I repeated, more out of a sense of relief.

Nigel, followed by Fern and Mike, walked towards me. When they were about twenty feet away, I turned and walked down the centre of Percy Street, which was free of ice, towards the clubhouse.

"Come on, Nigel," I said softly. "Come on, buddy," I repeated, snapping my finger and thumb together. "Come on, buddy." We passed through the intersection of Lisgar and Percy, I continued snapping my finger and thumb. As we drew abreast of the rear fire exit of the clubhouse, I felt a small cold hand slip into mine. We were soon bathed in the bright, warm glow of light that spilled from the clubhouse windows. Without saying anything we walked into the clubhouse, past all his excited chums in the hallway, and into my office. Finally our eyes met. Nigel gave me a warm smile, which indicated he was okay.

Reunited with his parents, and following an interview by the police, Nigel was soon in the safety of his home.

His one-eyed abductor was arrested.

Through a number of court appearances, over several years, Nigel and I developed a special bond.

Nigel continued to use the Boys and Girls Club for another twelve years as a member, volunteer and alumnus.

Had it not been for Barry, who remained alert and calm in a difficult situation; Mike and Fern, who backed me up without hesitation; and Nigel's presence of mind, this story may have had a very tragic conclusion.

Abducted

Seven-year-old saved by Boys' Club head

By DAVE McKAY
Journal Reporter

A seven-year-old boy was abducted at 9 p.m. Friday when he was picked up on Gloucester Street by a man driving a truck, police said.

The boy's 10-year-old brother — with whom he had been tobogganing — ran to the Ottawa Boys' Club on Nepean Street and told the director Bernard Muzeen what had occurred.

The boy then ran home and told his parents the licence number of the vehicle while Mr. Muzeen searched the neighborhood for the vehicle. He found a truck parked behind the Rideau Curling Club at Percy and Cooper Streets.

Inside were the boy and a man.

Mr. Muzeen told police he banged at the driver's window and demanded he release the boy, saying the boy was his son.

The driver put his vehicle into gear and roared off, dragging along the director who was holding onto the truck's door handle.

Mr. Muzeen managed to hold on for only a short distance and fell to the roadway. The driver of the truck drove on a few blocks and threw the child out.

Detectives Desmond Sloan and Bill Cathcart, following up leads, arrested a suspect in Manotick shortly after the abduction.

No charges have yet been laid.

The child — whom police would not identify — was not seriously injured.

Commentary:

- The text of Nigel's Rescue is based on my testimony in court.
- The newspaper account of this event is based on a brief statement released by the City of Ottawa police. The Club's legal counsel instructed me to refrain from any media interviews or commentary for the following reasons: Public statements could jeopardize any subsequent court case against the accused; and the publicity generated could lead some members of the general public to conclude that this little boy had been abducted from the Club.
- Nigel and I have never ever discussed this incident.
- Neither of us needed to say anything. We just knew how we felt about each other.
- Nigel experienced a traumatic period during the court trials and appeals procedures, which he passed through successfully, thanks to a loving family and the support of the Boys and Girls Club members.
- Some sixteen years later, I had the distinct pleasure of attending Nigel's wedding.
- When I last contacted this special friend, he was the proud father of two daughters and a son.

JAKE'S RESCUE

Inconceivably, there was a remarkable postscript to "Nigel's Rescue." It occurred some ten or twelve years later. I saw it as "Jake's Rescue" from his real and/or imaginary fears.

It all started when I was jarred into the realization that there was a commotion going on outside my office door.

"You get into Bernie's office right now, Jake," an adult voice commanded.

"Make me. I'd like to see you make me?" a child challenged.

"Jake, I'm telling you for the last time. Get into Bernie's office, right now." There was a brief pause then the adult voice threatened, "I'll have Bernie come and get you himself. Is that what you want, Jake?"

"I don't care," the child retorted.

"Come on, Jake, move. We have had enough of you today." There was frustration in the adult's voice.

Jake was a hyperactive nine-year-old boy, with the face of a cherub, a likeable disposition, strong self-will and a very short attention span.

He was well known to me and usually responded readily to my direction. In fact, he was one of the club members included in my guidance caseload.

I walked to the office door and observed Jake sitting on the floor of the lobby with both arms securely wrapped around the left leg of Marko, the gym supervisor. The upper part of Jake's body was against the other leg in such a way that he effectively immobilized Marko.

"Jake. Do I have to carry you?" Marko demanded, as he looked down at the child.

"I don't care," the tousle-haired boy responded.

Clearing my throat, I got their attention. "What don't you care about, Jake?"

Marko shook his head slowly and pointed both his hands towards the boy at his feet. It was an unspoken gesture of frustration.

Jake fixed me with a sweet smile. He supported his back against the right leg of his adult protagonist.

"Hi, Jake. Come here, buddy," I beckoned.

"No," he snapped back, a pout on his face.

"Oh, come on, buddy. Tell me what happened," I asked soothingly.

"No. No!" he yelled, as he looked around the clubhouse lobby. I felt that he was trying to gauge the amount of attention he had attracted.

Stepping away from the office doorway, I gestured for Jake to enter. To my surprise, he scampered to his feet and darted down an adjacent corridor towards the boys' locker room.

"Come here right now, Jake," I said softly, but firmly.

The boy stopped his headlong run. He turned and took several paces in my direction. Then with a big grin, he scampered into the locker room, glancing several times over his shoulder to observe my reaction.

I walked over to the doorway of the locker room. "Jake, you are not in any trouble," I assured him.

Folding my arms across my chest, I leaned against the doorframe.

The boy adopted a similar pose as he stood, with his back against the wall across the room from me. A broad smile lit up his face. His eyes danced with excitement.

After several moments I snapped my finger and thumb and pointed to the bench in front of me.

"No . . . no," the boy replied.

"How come, Jake? You're not scared of little old me?" I joked.

"Yeah . . . er, I guess so," was his tentative response.

"Come on. I thought we were buddies, Jake."

"Don't care." He looked around, as if trying to find another way out of the room.

"Hi, big guy, what are you doing here?" Nigel asked me in his deep resonant voice. He was on another of his frequent visits to the clubhouse as an alumnus and volunteer.

"I am waiting for Jake," I responded, without taking my eyes off the object of my attention.

"Why won't he come?" Nigel inquired.

"He says he is afraid of me."

"You're kidding. Who's scared of *you*, Bernie?" Nigel asked, as he broke into a big grin.

Nigel stepped into the locker room and walked towards the boy. For his part, Jake headed for the entrance of the shower room. Jake disappeared into the shower room. Nigel followed.

Several minutes passed. The sound of whispered conversation, which was unfortunately inaudible, drifted from the shower room.

Following a few moments of silence, a tiny hand came into view. It was followed by the boy's face with an eager expression. In an instant both disappeared and reappeared in the doorway. He seemed to be playing peekaboo.

Finally Jake's whole body came into view. Taking several steps towards me, he stopped and looked over his shoulder.

The boy listened attentively to whispered instructions. Smiling broadly, he walked over to where I stood.

Jake placed his little left hand into my extended right hand.

"The next time I call you, young man, you will come to me. Is that understood?" I asked.

The boy nodded his head in agreement. He had a sweet angelic smile on his upturned face.

"The reason why you must come to me, when I call you, is because I am your problem solver. If any club members or staff are unfair or bug you, please let me know. Jake, if you don't come how can I help you? Do you understand?" I asked, as I patted his shoulder.

He just stood there looking up at me. It was as if he had not heard a word I had said.

Shaking my arm vigorously, Jake asked, "Did you?" he fixed me with his dark brown eyes.

"Did I what?"

"Did you do what he said? Did you Bernie?" he turn and pointed to Nigel, who had by now emerged from the shower room.

I looked over to where Nigel stood. He had a mischievous smile on his face.

"If he said I did something. I guess I must have done it," I said choking up, as I returned my attention back to Jake.

Patting the boy on the head, I sent him on his way to the club.

The next thing I realized was that Nigel was standing beside me.

"What did you say to him?" I inquired.

"None of your business," he gave me a knowing grin. Nigel then gave me a bear hug the likes of which I have never received, before or since.

Thanks to Nigel's intervention, we had taken an important step in rescuing Jake from the fears that inhibited his social skills, abilities and integration.

Commentary:

- Jake's relationship with me greatly improved as he continued to participate and develop in the programs and services of the Boys and Girls Club.

- There is a temptation to isolate or separate hyperactive youngsters from the mainstream community. That course of action will deprive us of opportunities for the mutual acceptance, enrichment and integration of our social/community well being.

BREATH OF LIFE

Note: Only the name of the victim has been changed for his protection.
    All other names are real.

"Someone . . . Mr. Muzeen! Come quick!" my secretary called from the lower landing of the main stairwell of the Centre Town Clubhouse.

"What is it, Eileen? What is wrong?" I asked, as I leaned over the railing of the main floor landing.

"It's Claude. There's something seriously wrong down here," she responded, gesturing towards the basement door.

"What did you say? What's wrong?" I asked as I descended the flight of stairs to where Eileen stood.

"Claude's lying on the floor. I don't know what has happened," she explained as I passed by her.

I proceeded down the final flight two steps at a time. Through the open doorway of the basement workshop, I could see Claude. He lay on the floor among wood chips and sawdust. A quick scan of the prone figure showed an absence of blood.

Claude lay motionless. His face and lips lacked colour. There was white foam at the corner of his partially opened mouth.

Looking over my shoulder I said as calmly as possible "Eileen, please call for an ambulance. I will require the portable oxygen unit and some additional assistance."

Summoning up all my years of first aid training and practice I dropped to my knees beside Claude, determined to do whatever was necessary to help.

Placing my left ear close to Claude's mouth while scanning his chest for signs of movement, I hoped that all would be well. But there was no sound or sign of breathing.

Feeling very alone, I said a silent prayer that it was not too late; and furthermore, that I would remember all the Scout, RLSS, Red Cross, and St. John's Ambulance training taken over many years.

"Where the hell is that ambulance? Someone, please bring down that oxygen unit," I called in the direction of the stairwell, to anyone who could hear me.

There was no reply. I was on my own.

Wiping the foam from the mouth of my friend and co-worker with my handkerchief, I placed my left hand on Claude's forehead and the other on his chin to open his mouth. It was at that moment that I realized his false teeth were missing.

A quick glance around the workshop table and floor showed no sign of the missing teeth.

Peering between the slightly parted lips the corner of one set of teeth could be seen. "Damn! His teeth are stuck in his throat. That's why he's not breathing!" I said out loud to myself.

Applying additional pressure on Claude's chin, I was able to open his mouth just enough to reach in with my long finger. With some effort I was able to hook it around the nearest plate. I pulled gently, in an attempt to lift it out. To my great surprise it would not move. Feeling around, I discovered that the upper plate was wedged against the back of the mouth by the lower plate.

I was now in a cold sweat.

Determinedly, I hooked the long finger of my right hand around the upper plate and pulled firmly. It moved slightly. I pulled once again only to feel a searing pain rush through the finger that was in Claude's mouth. It was caused when his jaws snapped shut like a vice once the plates were dislodged.

Depressing the chin I released my sore finger along with the first of the entrapped false teeth plates. Retrieving the second plate from Claude's throat was not too difficult.

Wiping Claude's lips once more I proceeded to administer mouth-to-mouth resuscitation.

"Come on, Claude," I begged after five breaths. "Come on!"

I repeated the process a second time. Claude responded on the third "breath of life." Placing my left ear near his open mouth, I could hear my friend breathing rather laboriously. There was a slight gagging noise.

"You will be okay, Claude. Come on, buddy . . . BREATHE . . . please," I urged my unconscious co-worker.

"Can I help?" asked a soft male voice from behind. I felt a firm hand gently pressing on my right shoulder. "What can I do to help?" said a teenager who had now knelt to my right.

"Sure. Please go up to the office. Get the portable oxygen tank and bring it here." As the teenager got up to do my bidding, I tapped his leg and added "Tell Eileen that Claude had stopped breathing. Ask her to hurry up with that ambulance . . . please."

"Sure, I'll be right back," he assured me.

A wave of relief swept over me. I did not feel so alone any more.

"You'll be fine, Claude. Just stay with me. Come on, buddy . . . BREATHE!" Claude had opened his eyes slightly.

"The oxygen is here," the teen reported.

"Great. Set it up next to his head, please."

"Okay," the young man replied with a clear confident tone to his voice.

I found his presence to be most comforting and reassuring.

Claude moved his head and hand slightly. "Hold it there, Claude. You will be all right. Just stay still. Eileen has phoned for an ambulance. Keep your head still. We have to place the oxygen mask on your mouth. It will help you breathe better," I explained to my now semi-conscious co-worker.

The teenager tested the face mask from the oxygen tanks and then handed it to me. I placed it over Claude's mouth while my assistant adjusted the straps on Claude's head.

The intake of oxygen had an immediate effect, colour quickly returned to his lips . . . he moaned . . . and opened his eyes. I was now confident that we had been able to stabilize Claude's condition until professional assistance arrived.

"What is your name?" I asked my assistant at last.

"Tim."

"What are you doing here? Is today not a school day?"

"It sure is. I have a spare. I came in to see Jim. I have applied for the lifeguard position. I'm sorry but I came early to drop off my application form," Tim explained.

"We're not sorry, are we Claude?" I asked as we returned our attention to the man lying on the floor.

"Now, now, leave the equipment alone," I said gently as we both intercepted Claude's right hand that was trying to reach the oxygen mask.

Tim set about loosening Claude's shirt buttons, shoelaces, belt, and shirt cuffs.

Claude started to make sounds as if trying to talk.

"Tim, please go back upstairs and get me the blanket from the First Aid Unit. Also ask Eileen to find out when we can expect the ambulance," I requested.

Alone once more with my gravely ill friend and colleague of over ten years, time seemed to come to a standstill. I remained on my knees with my back to the stairwell.

"It's okay now," I repeated, more to reassure myself than my semi-conscious friend.

The quiet was broken by the sound of hard-soled shoes running down the steel-tipped stairs.

"My God, what do we have here?" said a strange voice. It turned out to be a member of the adult physical fitness club that was assembling in the main gymnasium for their noon-hour exercise session.

A heavy hand fell on my right shoulder as the stranger steadied himself and stepped over Claude's legs.

He dropped a grey blanket with red trim on the floor, to my right. Placing his clasped hands on Claude's chest he started to press up and down. It was not until the third pressing movement that I was able to recover my wits and react to this unexpected intervention.

My training had taught me that only one person is in charge of an emergency, and that all support personnel should ask how they could be of assistance. Consequently, I challenged the stranger. "What the hell do you think you are doing?"

"Heart massage. You know CPR?" he replied.

"Claude has a breathing problem. Leave him alone," I waved the stranger's hands away from Claude's chest. "You can place that blanket over him, if you really want to be helpful."

Claude started to move his head once more. He muttered and started to open and close his eyes.

"I will have Eileen let Jeannette know all about this. We will also tell her to which hospital the ambulance will take you . . . okay?"

Claude closed his eyes and gave a muffled grunt from behind the oxygen mask. His right hand tapped my arm. I took his hand in mine and he gave a firm squeeze.

"The ambulance is here," Eileen announced from behind me.

"How's Claude?" she asked anxiously, as she had preceded the ambulance attendants into the workshop.

"We have him breathing on his own. Thank God. I'm sure he's going to be okay," was my prayerful response.

The clattering in the stairwell indicated to one and all that the ambulance attendants had arrived. Once they had set up their equipment they relieved me of the responsibility of looking after Claude.

I suddenly felt very cold and found myself shaking. More from relief than fear.

Once the ambulance attendants moved in to treat Claude, I stood up. My knees hurt. It was not until I brushed off my pants legs that I realized I had been kneeling on wood chips that littered the floor of the maintenance room.

I learned later that before Tim returned to school, he had asked the "CPR man" to bring the first aid kit blanket down to me.

Claude made a full recovery and several months later he was back at work at the clubhouse.

Jeannette and Claude's daughter came to the clubhouse to thank me for my prompt response. I also got to see his first grandchild.

In the months and years that followed there was a special warmth and gentleness in our relationship. This was due in great part to the joys and delights of grandfatherhood that a "breath of life" provided to Claude.

In all the years that I have both taken and taught the Rescue Breathing Course I never expected to be faced with a real-life situation.

When I recount this event I shudder to think what would have happened to Claude or myself if I had not been trained in giving the **breath of life**.

Commentary:

- There is a need to have as many citizens as possible trained in lifesaving, CPR, first aid, rescue skills, and mouth-to-mouth resuscitation. It should be considered as an investment in the welfare of the community as a whole.

- Consideration should be given to providing incentives or credits to high school, community college and university students to learn and develop these emergency skills.

- The Scouts Canada motto "Be Prepared" has enabled me to have the skills to assist others in times of distress.

- I hope and pray that if ever I am in need of such assistance, the individual who arrives on the scene will be able to help.

A SHOT IN THE PARK

NOTE: The names of the young participants have been changed for their protection.

Harry Johnson, the front desk clerk, became indisposed and had gone home early. It fell to me to assume his duties.

The senior Club members were more interested in playing baseball in the park, across the street from our Ottawa Boys Club, as it was known in the early '70s, than relieving me from staffing the front desk.

Checking in members, answering the telephone, providing change for the vending machine and registering youngsters for the upcoming summer program kept me and my self-appointed assistant, eleven-year-old Richard, quite busy.

It must have been about 7:40 p.m. I was on the telephone with the parent of a Club member who was seeking information about our summer program when six teenagers came in.

"Numbers, guys?" my young assistant asked.

Warren, Perry, Shawn, Guy, Jean and Bert ignored his request. They scurried in single file across the front hall and up the stairs. The sullen expression on their faces alerted me to the possibility that something was seriously wrong.

"Bernie, those guys didn't check in. Do you want me to get them to come back and sign in?" Richard asked.

"Eh . . . er . . . no, thank you," I said, as I hung up the telephone receiver.

"Shall I mark them in as members or visitors?" Richard asked, his pencil poised over the daily sign-in sheet.

"Write in four seniors and two intermediate members," I responded, and prepared the intercom to talk to the guidance counsellor.

"Hi, Rob. I think we have trouble!"

"Oh. What is it?" Rob inquired.

"I don't really know. It was the way Warren, Perry and the other guys came in, I think—"

"He has just walked into my office," the guidance counsellor interjected. "Will call you back, if there is anything to it. Okay?"

The intercom went dead.

"Sure," I muttered.

The waning sun forced the baseball players back into the clubhouse, some twenty minutes later. After some good-natured give and take with them, I authorized that the swimming pool could remain open for an extra half hour so they could have a quick dip.

"Come on, make it an hour, Bernie," D'Arcy insisted.

"You guys had—" the buzzing of the intercom interrupted me in mid-sentence. "Hold it, guys." I picked up the receiver.

"I think you had better get up here, Bernie," Rob advised, in his low monotone voice.

"Just give me a moment to lock up the cash and valuables. Okay?" I said into the intercom.

"Just a moment, please." I covered the mouthpiece of the receiver and turned my attention back to the baseball players, who were milling around me.

"Okay, guys. It's half an hour swim or nothing."

They let out a cheer and headed to the locker room.

"D'Arcy, would you please let Pierre know that I have asked that the pool be open an extra hour for these guys. I mean, a half hour."

"Sure Bernie."

"And D'Arcy, please tell the lifeguard that I will be tied up for the next little while," I added.

Upon entering Rob's office, a room he shared with John, the group services coordinator, I came face to face with the group that had entered the clubhouse earlier. They seemed to be in a glum mood.

Sitting on the edge of John's desk, I was faced by Warren. In a row behind, were Perry, Shawn, Jean and Bert. Standing behind all of them was Guy. I knew each of these club members, some since they were six years of age.

Several of the youngsters cleared their throats in nervous anticipation. Several stole quick glances at me. The tension was broken when Rob asked, "Well guys, who is going to tell Bernie what happened?"

All six heads snapped around to look at my co-worker. He was sitting at his desk, across the room from me.

"Come on. How about you, Warren . . . " he trailed away.

"Yes. Sure," the boy sighed.

Warren made eye contact with me. He flashed a forced smile, took a deep breath and in a voice that was remarkably calm, shared the following incident.

"Us guys and Larry, well we went down to the park."

"Excuse me, Warren. Where is Larry?" I asked, looking around the room.

"He took off," Guy volunteered.

"What's this park are you referring to?" I added.

"The park behind the hotel, next to Parliament Hill," replied fourteen-year-old Shawn.

"Major Hill Park?" I asked.

"Yes. Well in that park, us guys decided to roll a feller and take his money. You know, everyone does it." Warren paused, as if waiting for a reaction from Rob or me.

"Anyway, after the guys hid in the bushes and I got this feller to come over to me, they all jumped him and tackled him to the ground. Well, this particular feller put up a fight. Larry got real mad at him and put the boots to his head. The man stopped fighting. Perry searched the feller for his wallet and money. While doing that he found one of those small leather things, with a police badge in it," said Warren.

"It was not a police badge, but one for one of those security guys, I think," sixteen-year-old Perry interjected.

"Well, whatever. Larry decided that if this guy was a cop he must have a gun. He found it, here," Warren pointed the left side of his chest, just below the armpit.

"Some of us were not sure it was real. Larry took the gun and raised it in the air and pulled the trigger. Man it made a hell of a bang. Scared us all. Eh, fellows?"

Heads nodded in agreement.

"Everyone must have heard it," he paused and took deep breath.

"We got the hell out of there, and fast," Guy added.

"Where did you go, fellows?" Rob prompted.

"Right here," Perry exclaimed.

"And where is the gun?" I asked, in a matter of fact tone, hoping they did not have it with them.

"He kept it," Bert whispered.

"Who?"

"Larry. Larry kept it, Bernie," Warren stated, after clearing his throat.

A wave of relief swept over me.

Shaking my head, I realized that we, the Club members, Rob and I, were faced with a serious predicament. I was conscious that whatever I said, and the manner in which I said it, could have a profound effect on all concerned.

"Er, fellows, is the floor more attractive than my face?" All through Warren's explanation, only he had looked at me.

A few bemused smiles crossed the youngsters' faces. The comment seemed to relax them a little.

"Each and every one of you knows right from wrong," I started slowly. Shaking my head, I continued. "I just don't understand how any of you could be involved in such . . . er . . . in such an act," I took the time to look into the face of each boy. "I am truly shocked. Do you realize how serious this is?" I paused for effect. "Larry, who is not here, fired a gun within sight of the Parliament of Canada. Think about it."

During a long pause they shifted their weight, indicating their discomfort.

"Bernie, these guys know they have got themselves into serious trouble," Rob interjected. "They don't need to hear all this from you. Not now."

Perry turned to Rob and said, "We're used to knowing what Bernie feels and thinks when we screw up."

Perry made eye-to-eye contact with me for the first time since I entered Rob's office. He licked his upper lip, nervously.

Perry held eye contact as he asked in an even tone of voice. "What we need to know, Bernie, is what can we do about this whole thing?" He raised an eyebrow, questioningly.

"Perry, you and your friends have committed a very serious crime. I appreciate that you have turned to Rob and me for advice. That shows us that you wish to do the right thing. But in doing so you have made both of us accessories after the fact." I scanned the upturned faces.

"What's that . . . er . . . accessories thing?"

"Perry, if you guys choose to do nothing about what happened this evening, the law requires that Rob and I must report what we know to the authorities. There's no way of getting around it. That is the law," I said, without shifting my gaze from Perry.

"What's that accessory . . . eh, thing?" Shawn asked.

"They are in big trouble if they do nothing about it, man," Perry explained, somewhat impatiently, to the younger boy who sat to his left.

"Right, Perry," I said. I paced back and forth in front of the group.

"Let me tell you what I am going to do. I leave the club at about 9:30 p.m. That's about thirty-five minutes from now," I glanced at my watch. "On my way home I have to pass Waller Street, where the police station is located. It is my intention to stop in there and share with the police the information you have provided me."

Guy let out an audible sigh.

I said, "Guy, what do you think they will do following my visit?"

"The cops? They will come to our houses and arrest us," a tear rolled down his cheek. He pressed his lips together, trying to retain his composure.

"But if you guys went to the police station on your own and told them what happened, in particular the firing of the gun, that might indicate to the police, courts, and your families that you are not all bad. Fellows, you have to remember that when giving the police information about that shooting, you will have to admit that you were involved in an assault."

A loud sniffling filled the room.

"What the police reaction to such an admission would be I just cannot predict. I'm sorry." I paused to let the point sink in. "However, I think I can predict that at any trial, the judge would look favourably on your action of going on your own to the police. It would show that none of you had anything to do with that gun. As I see it, you could all be charged with assault and robbery—maybe even armed robbery, seeing that a gun was involved. It is so hard to say . . ." I trailed off, at a loss for words.

I was determined not to solve their problem for them by telling them what to do. Given that they would have to suffer the consequences of their action, it was up to each one of them to decide which option they would follow. In the meantime, I wanted to leave no doubt in their minds as to the course of action I intended to pursue.

"Now you guys know what I am going to do. It is really up to each and every one of you to decide what to do, whether you do it as a group, with your parents, or individually. Know that whatever you decide, I will be there to support and help you," I added, as I headed for the door.

Coughing cleared a number of young throats. They now realized that they were faced with a moment of truth.

"I am so sorry there is nothing more I can do to help these guys right now, Rob." I struggled to keep my emotions in check. "Of course, one of us could take that decision away from them by telephoning the police and have them come here and pick them up," I threw out for a reaction.

"No. Don't. Please, Bernie," Warren urged, face flushed.

Turning around I leaned against the door. "Okay. It took guts for you six guys to come in here and tell Rob and me about what you did. If you can tell us, then it should not be difficult for you to tell your parents, the police, and maybe a judge in court. Warren, you and your friends are asking me to take a big risk. How do I know that you guys will not take off? But I will take that risk. Okay?" I extended my right hand in his direction.

"Where would we go? We've got no money," Perry said, more to his friends than to me, as he walked over and shook my hand.

"Thanks, Bernie." "Er, sorry." "Let's go, guys," was the mixed response of these Club members.

* * *

I entered the police station at 9:35 p.m. Placing my business card on the counter I started to tell the officer about the shot in the park.

He motioned me to stop talking by raising the palm of his hand up in the air, as though directing traffic.

"We know all about it, sir," he advised.

"I can provide you with the names, addresses and phone numbers of those involved," I volunteered.

"Thank you sir, but six young people surrendered themselves a short while ago."

Biting my lower lip, I was at a loss as to whether I should cheer or cry. Warren and his friends had decided to face up to what they had done.

After several deep breaths to maintain my composure, I said, "Officer, I have learned that there was an older teenager who took and fired the gun." The officer nodded his head knowingly.

"You will be pleased to know, sir, that we have recovered the gun, thanks to the information provided to us earlier," he added in a matter-of-fact tone of voice.

"Have you been able to take Larry J. into custody, Officer?"

"Not at the present time, sir."

It was with mixed feelings that I turned and walked towards the front door of the police station. However, curiosity drew me back.

"Excuse me, Officer. May I inquire as to what has happened to Warren and the other boys who surrendered?"

"Four of them are in the cells below. The two juveniles were taken to the Youth Detention Centre, on Bronson Avenue."

As if reading my mind, the policeman added, "The adults will be arraigned in court on Monday morning. About 9:30 a.m., I would guess."

"Well, that's that." I turned and headed for the front door.

"Good night, sir," the officer said, in a loud clear voice.

I turned in his direction; he gave me a broad smile with the "thumbs up" sign. "They will be fine. I would say that they will be back at the Boys Club real soon," he volunteered.

"Thanks! Good night, Officer," I waved.

Commentary:

- Larry was picked up later that night. All seven were bound over to stand trial.

- About a year was to pass before this matter was brought before the courts.

- In the intervening time Warren, Perry, Shawn, Guy, Jean and Bert excelled at school, attended the Boys Club regularly, undertook community service projects and were co-operative at home. They clearly demonstrated that each one of them had the potential to be good, contributing citizens.

- The result of their trial was a long term of probation.

- Recent contacts and information show that the six club members have gone on, with differing degrees of success, to complete their education, get married, have children and prosper in the business of their choice.

- As for Larry, he too got married and had a family. However, I am sorry to say that his continued antisocial/criminal behaviour has resulted in several terms of imprisonment.

Alternatives:

Recent data indicates that it costs about $250 to $400 per year to insure the participation of each child or youth in the wide range of social, educational, recreational and guidance activities at a Boys and Girls Club.

Compare those costs to the $16,000 to $20,000 per year to imprison an adult—or $20,000 to $25,000 for a juvenile—in detention or treatment centres.

There is no doubt in my mind that the guidance, recreational, social and cultural activities of the Boys and Girls Club movement are truly an investment in the nation's most precious, renewable resource for the future: **our children and youth.**

When given the opportunity, most young people tend to want to do the correct thing following an antisocial incident.

Leaders need to learn how to provide youth with space, opportunity and support when they take responsibility for their own actions and behaviour. This does not mean that youth are to be indulged in their wrongdoing or allowed to escape being held accountable for their individual actions.

THE HIT AND RUN

To finalize the executive director's report for the sixty-second annual general meeting of the board of directors of the Boys and Girls Club of Ottawa–Carleton, I dropped by my office on a quiet Sunday afternoon.

"Hello!" I said answering the telephone after it had rung seven times.

"Bernie . . . !"

"Yes."

"Bernie, there has been a hit and run," the breathless voice of a child stated.

"Is anyone hurt?"

"Yes!" he exclaimed.

"Who is this, please?" I asked, picking up a pencil.

"Billy, over at the project," was the response.

"Do you know who was hurt?"

"Yes. My dog Lady."

"Oh, Billy! This is not funny, my young friend. You almost had me hang up on you so I could call the police!" was my stern reply.

"But Bernie, there was a hit and run. Two guys were in a blue car that hurt Lady," my caller mumbled. "If I see them again shall I call you?" he asked.

"Hold it, Billy! If you ever see them again tell your mum and let her call the police. Is your mum home, Billy"?

"No. She's out shopping."

"Do you need me to come over and look after your pet?"

"No thanks. Mrs. Williams, who lives next door, she saw it all. She wrapped Lady in my jacket and took her to the animal hospital."

"Oh, that's good news. Billy, will you telephone me and let me know if your pet is okay? I expect to be here until about 4:30 p.m."

"Sure."

"Now, Billy. Can you give me some details as to where this hit and run occurred so that I can report it to the police?"

"Just a moment."

Through the telephone I could hear a muffled conversation.

"Hi, Bernie! Mrs. Jordan, who also saw it all, has already called the police."

"Will you be staying with Mrs. Jordan until your mother returns from shopping?"

"Yeah!"

"Billy, I hope that it all works out for Lady. So take it easy."

"See you at the Club next Saturday, Bernie."

"Sure thing. Goodbye!"

I felt really good that this Club member sought support and comfort from our organization, in a time of personal stress and need.

Commentary:

- Three days later I telephoned Billy and learned that Lady had been returned home.
- Within the month Lady had to be put down.
- The fact that Billy felt he could turn to his Boys and Girls Club in this moment of personal crisis must have been of comfort.

PART III

Guidance & Behaviour Modification

A WORD TO THE WISE

In a total of forty years of volunteer and professional service of providing guidance, counselling, advice, and leadership to children and youth I have found it necessary and helpful to have a number of insights, observations, opinions, explanations, and points of view regarding issues that impact on the day-to-day lives of those placed in my care.

The following are some examples offered for the reader's consideration:

Fair Play
> To play fair is admirable . . .
> To play fair and to win is exceptional . . .
> To play fair and to lose gracefully is a sign of courage.

Good Sport
> A good sport is more interested in winning friends than in winning games.

Being Honest
> It's better to be honest than to be a cheat.
> It is a much greater challenge to be honest to oneself than to others.
> Be honest to yourself, others, and group—in that order.

Being Kind
> Kindness works similar to an infection—it can spread care, hope, love, dignity, opportunity, joy . . .

It's Their Life
> As much as you may wish to eliminate the difficulties of loved ones or dear friends, please remember: *You cannot live their life for them.*

It's Your Destiny
> When you encounter challenge, opportunity, temptation, danger, success, or triumphs in life, remember: *You are the master/mistress of your own destiny.*

Friends
> Pals come and go, but one good friendship can last a lifetime . . .
> I prefer to have one good friend than to have 100 pals . . .
> A friend in need is a friend indeed . . .
> A real friend serves as a mirror that offers a true reflection in times of challenge and triumph.

Differences
> Differences between people can be minor, but unbridgeable . . .
> A difference between two people can be vast but bridged with good will and trust . . .

A difference of opinion is often a matter of perspective . . .
Don't let differences get in the way of positive relationships . . .
The difference between "like" and "dislike" is mostly attitude . . .
It is quite acceptable to look different . . . hold a different point of view
. . . have a different set of values . . . hold a different faith.

Sharing Skills

To share your skill and ability in life or a sport can provide someone
with the capability to perform better than you.
Sharing a skill encourages independence and expresses your own self-
confidence.
When sharing a skill remember with kindness the person who took the
time to teach it to you.

Foul Language

Users of foul language show their own ignorance.
Use of foul language indicates a lack of self-respect.
Foul language underscores a lack of self-confidence.
Verbal abuse can result in breaking a victim's spirit.
Foul language is a form of verbal pollution that only individual action
can eliminate for the good of society.
Verbal abuse can leave serious scars that last a lifetime.

Drugs

Medications heal but drugs can maim and kill.
Life is more enjoyable when one remains drug-free.
There is no such thing as "free drugs," given that your first and only
encounter of such substances could cost you your life.

Education

It's better to stay in school for one year, and be taught by a teacher you
don't like, than to quit school and endure many unhappy years of a life
you don't like.
Education/learning is a never-ending process in life.
The young can learn from their elders . . .
The young can teach their elders . . .
The elderly, and young, teach others by example.
The more you learn, the more you discover how little you actually
know.

Truth

Truth serves as a mantle and shield in times of difficulty.
To tell the truth without hesitation takes courage and indicates a sense
of self-assurance that is admirable.
Truth-telling has a profound healing effect on the aggrieved.

Truth is a priceless component of trust . . . love . . . friendship . . . affection . . . business . . .

Lies

Lies are an "epidemic" that poison relationships . . . scare one's mind, heart, and soul . . . fester and inflict pain . . . and are extremely difficult to sustain without telling additional lies.

A QUESTION OF COMPREHENSION

Note: Only the names of the central characters have been changed for their protection.

Friday, 12th of August.

The clubhouse was quiet, at last. The children, volunteers and staff were gone for a three-week holiday break, now that the summer program was completed.

The task at hand for me was to track down an error in the computerized midyear financial statements. It was a task that had to be completed, regardless of the amount of time it took, before I could get away for my own vacation.

The rattling of the front door of the clubhouse broke the silence and my train of thought. A glance at the radio clock on my desk indicated that it was 6:23 p.m.

I chose to ignore the temptation to go to the door. After all, there was a large sign on the front door announcing that the clubhouse would be closed for the next three weeks. *If I do nothing*, I thought, *hopefully whoever it is will go away.*

My concentration returned to the computerized sheets spread out before me on the worktable.

Several minutes later the rattling of the front door became very intense. It was as if someone was trying to pull the doors out of their frames.

Fuming, I strode into the front hall and stood where I could be seen by whoever was outside.

It was Camino.

"What the hell do you think you're doing, Camino? Can't you read the sign in front of you?" I shouted, so as to be heard through the two sets of doors. This to some extent released my feeling of annoyance at being distracted from the important work at hand.

Camino dejectedly turned away from the door. Making his way down the four steps in front of the building he stopped and sat down, and brought both hands to his face.

After taking a few paces towards my office I was overcome by guilt and I turned around and headed for the door. I just cannot explain why.

"Camino, Camino, what do you want?" I asked, as I poked my head outside the front door.

"A drink of water, please," he mumbled.

"Well, you have got me here. You might as well come in now," I said.

He brushed past me. I fiddled with the key in the lock.

"Jim and the gang are away for the next three weeks. In fact, I should be on my way, but I have this budget problem to resolve," I explained in a matter-of-fact manner as I reset the door lock.

Turning around, I found Camino, a nineteen-year-old who looked four years younger, sobbing so hard that his whole body shook. Tears streamed down his face.

"Calm down, Camino. Things can't be that bad."

The young man waved his hand in the air. His attempt to talk was stifled by his emotional distress. Placing my hand in the middle of his back, I got him to start walking in the direction of my office.

"You go on into my office and sit down. I will get a couple of drinks. Okay?" I said, softly.

Camino waved his right arm in the air and nodded his head. It was clear that this young man was close to the emotional edge. Something dramatic, I thought, must be afoot.

I took my time getting the drinks in the hope that Camino would regain his composure.

Camino had been a Club member for about eight years. Recently, he had been volunteering with the disabled children's program and making a valuable contribution.

Basically a loner, he was the son of immigrant parents. Camino never completed grade ten. His parents, who had not learned either English or French, had difficulties in communicating with teachers, neighbours, and the workers of community agencies.

A quiet, gentle individual, Camino was not active in sports. He'd had his share of run-ins with individuals at his school and with clubhouse staff, over the years. But nothing too serious.

There were rumours that he was in conflict with the law.

"Well, Camino, you owe me another drink," I said, sliding his drink across the table.

He looked up at me and gave me a brief smile. The tears had stopped and he had regained his composure.

"Thanks," he said.

"Oh that's okay. Sorry I didn't let you in before. I'm trying to catch up with all this paperwork, before I go on holiday," I said, patting the pile of paper on the worktable.

"When are you going, Bernie?" he asked, after his first sip of the cold drink.

"Well, it will have to be tomorrow, I guess. Too late to take off tonight," I sighed as I sat in a chair on the other side of the table from my unexpected guest.

"I see," was Camino's response as he looked intently at his drink can.

"Well, are you going to tell me?" I asked.

"Tell you what?" he responded.

"Camino, come off it! When are you going to tell me why you are so upset?"

"It does not matter now, honest, Bernie." He raised both eyebrows and pressed his lips together.

"How many years have we known each other, my friend?"

"About eight, maybe nine years, I would say. Why?"

"In all that time, we have developed the knack of reading each other. Don't you agree, Camino?"

"Guess so. Pretty well." His face was contorted as if he were struggling to prevent the tears from flowing again.

"Camino, relax and tell me what's the problem. Why did you nearly pull the front doors off their hinges and that other stuff? Come on, my young friend. Please trust me. What's wrong?"

He gestured to the budget papers spread out on the worktable and sighed.

"Hey, forget all of that. I can finish the budget on Monday, if I have to. Let's see if, together, we can sort out what's troubling you?"

Camino nodded his head and then took a long slow drink out of the pop can. I placed all the budget papers in their portfolio.

Placing the can on the table, he slid it between his thumbs and index fingers.

"Did Jim tell you, Bernie?" He coughed, to clear his throat.

"Jim who? Tell me what? What are you talking about, Camino?"

"I came in to see Jim. I asked him to come to court and speak for me. He said he would be on holiday. So he was going to talk to you and see if you would go for me. But . . ." he trailed off.

"But what?"

"But you are on holiday too, I guess." Placing his elbows on the table, the young man buried his face in his hands. His body shook as he tried to suppress another bout of sobbing.

"Now you are my boss! First you're a Club member; then a teen leader; a volunteer; now you are trying to be my boss."

"What did I say?" the young man asked, with an astonished look on his tear-stained face.

"Telling me I'm on holiday. Just like a boss, Camino!" I exclaimed. "I already told you, I'll have to come in on Monday to finish up this budget. So relax. You're not stopping me from going on holiday. Okay?"

He smiled weakly and settled back in his red leather chair.

"Now, what did you tell Jim?"

"I told him that my lawyer has asked me to find someone to go to court next Tuesday. If I don't, he said I could go to jail."

"Who said that?"

"My lawyer."

"Why?"

"I don't really know. I didn't steal the stuff. It was Paul and Duke," he replied in all seriousness.

"Were you there, with them, when they stole the stuff?"

"Yeah. But only once."

"What kind of stuff did Paul and Duke steal?"

"Stereos, tape decks, speakers, controls and stuff, you know."

"From a house?"

"No, from stores," he said breathlessly.

"And you were there, Camino?"

He nodded in agreement.

"Doing what?"

"Nothing. Honest. I was just there. I didn't go in that place."

"Were you the lookout?"

"Well, er . . . Paul told me to call out if anyone came."

"Well, I guess the police came?"

"Oh no, Bernie." He raised his hand, as if to stop my train of thought.

"Then how come you are now before the courts? I just don't understand, Camino."

"Well, Duke had been ripping off this kind of stuff for a long time. The cops caught him. He told on me."

"Duke told the police that you were a lookout on one of his raids?"

"No. He told the cops that Paul and him had put some of the stuff at my place."

"Possession of stolen goods," I exclaimed.

"What?" Camino's brow became knitted.

"Unless your lawyer can tell me more, it would seem to me that you have been tried for 'possession of stolen goods.' That's what it is called. It is a very serious charge." I took a sip from my drink. "What does your lawyer say may be the outcome of the trial?"

"Oh that's all over, Bernie. My lawyer, he says I can get two years in jail if I don't have someone go to court on Tuesday." He dropped his chin on to his chest.

"When on Tuesday, Camino?"

"Ten-thirty in the morning," he mumbled.

"Why?"

"To talk to the judge, I guess." Camino renewed eye contact.

"Now, Camino, why us? Why the Club, why Jim, why me? I would like to understand." I gestured with my right hand. "Why should we go to court for you?"

"I don't know anyone else," he responded, wide-eyed.

"Your father? A teacher? An uncle?" To each of these alternatives this young man shook his head no.

He was all alone.

"Only you now, Bernie. Jim told me last Thursday that he was going away on holiday. Now maybe you will go . . ." It was more a question than a comment.

"Camino, you thank your lucky stars that the computer screwed up my mid-year budget. Otherwise I would not be here."

He playfully patted the portfolio of computer papers that lay on the table between us and smiled.

"Why did you not get in to see me before now? You have known about this since last Thursday?" I asked softly.

"I had to work overtime at my job. My boss would not let me have time off."

"Does he know why you wanted the time off?"

"Oh no, Bernie." He became tense.

"I understand. Now I see why you were so upset earlier. You have tried to handle this whole thing alone. Am I right, Camino?"

"Right," he exhaled a deep breath.

"Who is your lawyer?"

"I have his card here." He fumbled in his wallet. "Maybe you could call him?" Camino asked, offering a dog-eared business card.

"Not on a Friday night in August. I guess not."

I smiled as I made a note of the lawyer's name and telephone number before handing the card back. He was an alumnus of the Boys and Girls Club, well known to me as a Service Club member.

"Camino. You did wrong, okay?" I said, as I attempted to get to the heart of the problem.

"Not really. It was Paul and Duke who stole the stuff. I only kept it in my place, Bernie," my friend responded forcefully.

"Did they pay you to keep it?"

"No. It's their stuff."

"You really do not understand how serious this matter is, do you, Camino?"

"Oh, yes. My lawyer said I will go to jail for two years," he sighed.

"Should you go to jail?"

"No. I did not steal the stuff."

"Is that the only reason, Camino?"

"No. I heard of the kind of stuff they do to young guys in those places." He shivered.

"What do you expect me to say in court? If I go?" I asked, as I watched him closely.

Shaking his head, he responded, "I don't know . . ."

"I will have to tell the truth, and you know what it is!"

The young man slumped in his chair. A glum expression was on his face.

"Camino, the truth is that you know right from wrong; the truth is that you are a school dropout; the truth is that you do not have friends; the truth is you looked after stolen 'stuff' for Duke and Paul. You see the truth can be very negative."

I paused for a drink. Camino's lips moved, but no sound emerged.

"The truth is also that you have been a Club member for eight or nine years; the truth is that you are not a bad person; the truth is that you are not a troublemaker; the truth is that you volunteer to work with the disabled; the truth is that you co-operate with the clubhouse staff. As you can see Camino, the truth also has its positive aspects."

"What's that?"

"What's what, Camino?"

"That aspects, thing?"

"It means parts. The point I am making is that truth can be both good and bad. Should I get up in court, I will have to answer all the questions put to me, truthfully. Do you understand?"

"I know, Bernie"

"Can you trust me to do that? Do you really wish me to go to court knowing that I may have to say something that could be seen as being negative?"

"Oh, yes. I would like you there," he said.

"Camino, did you steal any of that stuff found in your home?"

"No!" he brought his hands down on the table with a bang. "Oh, I'm sorry," was his reflex response.

"That's okay. Now, what else can I tell the judge?"

"What do you mean?"

"Do I tell the judge that you will continue to look after stolen stuff? Do I tell him that you will continue to run with Duke and Paul and other troublemakers?"

"No. That is all over. I did not steal that stuff. I will not see Duke or Paul. I will be good. Honest, Bernie," Camino's eyes were dancing in his head, as if searching for the right things to say.

"Sounds good so far. Anything else you can think of, Camino?"

"Yes. I will help the disabled kids. I will come to the Club all the time. I will stay out of trouble. Bernie, I didn't steal that stuff, honest I didn't." Camino dropped his chin to his chest once more. He was clearly physically and emotionally exhausted.

"Can I tell the judge that no good will come from sending you to jail? Can I tell the judge that you are sorry? Can I tell the judge that you did not steal any of 'that stuff'? Can I tell the judge that you will help us at the Boys and Girls Club and that you will participate in regular meetings with our guidance staff?"

As I spoke Camino slowly lifted his head so that he was fully face to face with me. A light, bright smile was on his face.

"Sure Bernie," he responded breathlessly. "I will volunteer at the Club and do all those other things you said."

"How often?"

"What do you mean, Bernie?"

"How often—how many times a week will you volunteer?"

"Every day if you want."

"Camino, it is not what I want. It has to be what you are able to do. Remember, what I say has to not only be true, it has to be practicable. Okay?" I explained firmly.

"Sure, I see. Well, I can help the handicapped kids. I like that. Then I could run the games room and maybe help Kevin in the gym," he offered.

"Are you suggesting three evenings a week, once the clubhouse opens in September?"

"Yeah."

"I beg your pardon. 'Yeah,' what's that?"

"Sorry, I mean yes," he countered, with a shy smile.

"Do you realize that if the judge accepts your offer to serve as a volunteer at the clubhouse three times a week, it could become part of a Probation Order/Community Service Order that you will have to serve, without screwing up? Can you do it?"

"I think so, Bernie."

"Camino, 'think so' is not good enough. Damn it, don't you understand how serious this whole matter is?" I demanded, more in sorrow than in anger.

My young observer started to blink his eyes rapidly. A sure sign that he was getting all worked up once again. Reaching across the table, I tapped the back of his right hand. "Camino, look at me, please."

He lifted his head.

"I'm sorry, Camino. I want to be sure that you understand. You and I cannot screw up on any of this. It is serious business—so we have to be sure we get it right. You don't help things if you get upset when I push a point with you. It is not my intention or wish to hurt you," I explained.

"It's okay, Bernie." He licked his lips and took a deep breath.

"Good. Now, where were we?"

"Me volunteering here three times a week." He ran the back of his hand across his eyes. "Then there is that other stuff about being sorry and staying away from those other guys."

"Great. Well, there is not much more we can do now, on a Friday evening. Can you come in and see me on Monday morning?"

"Sure. I don't work on Mondays," he remarked, with a happy tone to his voice.

"Say nine a.m., here in my office," I proposed, as I stood up to get the daybook from my desk.

"Later, maybe?" he requested softly.

"Okay, let's say ten-thirty a.m.?"

Camino's smiling face provided the answer.

My young guest stood up and stretched. He then finished his drink and placed the empty can in the litter basket.

"Thanks, Bernie. I hope you didn't mind?"

"Not at all, Camino. That's what the Boys and Girls Club is here for. See you Monday?"

"Sure thing."

"At ten-thirty."

"I know," he said, with a playful tone in his voice. His right hand was extended in my direction.

We shook hands. I got the distinct feeling that our handshake was both firmer and longer than usual.

"Let's get out of here, guy. You go home have a good meal and a good night's sleep. As for me, I still have time for a swim before my beauty sleep."

"Ho yeah!"

We both laughed and headed for the front door. As we exited the clubhouse, Camino touched my elbow. "I just wanted to say thank you and sorry for . . . well, you know."

"For being upset. Don't think about it, my friend. Show up on Monday and stay out of trouble."

"Sure, I know. Thanks again, Bernie. Good night."

Driving home, I could not quite put my finger on what bothered me about Camino. Maybe I was too tired to figure it out.

Monday, 10:35 a.m.

"Hi. Can I come in?" the young man asked, with an expectant expression on his face.

"Hi, there. So you made it. Come on in and sit down," I said flatly.

Turning my attention to the midyear financial statements, some ten minutes must have elapsed before Camino asked, "Did you call the lawyer, Bernie?"

"Did I what?"

"Did you talk to my lawyer?" he ventured.

"No. Not yet. I figured I should wait for his client. By the way, Camino, you're late," I added sharply.

"I am?" he glanced at his watch.

"You are, believe me. How come?"

"Well, I stopped to talk to some guys on Somerset Street." He licked his lips.

"So tomorrow, will the judge and the court officials have to wait for you, while you stop to gab with your friends?"

He shrugged his shoulders.

"I still think that you don't realize how serious a situation you are in. Do you?"

"Well yeah!"

"Tell me."

"Tell you what?" Camino asked, with a puzzled expression on his face.

"Tell me how serious it is for you?"

"Well, I can go to jail for the stuff Paul and Duke took."

"No, no, no, my young friend. You really do not understand. Oh well, let's talk to your lawyer. Camino, are you going to court tomorrow dressed like that?" I asked as I dialled the lawyer's telephone number.

"Why not?" his eyebrows arched.

"We will talk about that—" I raised my hand as the telephone was answered.

"Hallo. This is Bernard Muzeen over at the Boys and Girls Club. I am calling in connection with Camino B. May I talk to Mr. Rossey, please?"

"Just a moment, sir," said a female voice.

"Hallo, Mr. Muzeen, how are you?" a familiar male voice asked.

"Fine, Mr. Rossey, and you?"

"Well, thank you."

"Larry, I understand that you are Camino B.'s lawyer?"

"That's correct, Bernie."

"Larry, I have Camino here in my office. He showed up on Friday evening and explained to me his present predicament. Camino is convinced that he will get two years in jail for something other people did. I have tried to explain that possession of stolen property is very serious."

"So have I. He just does not seem to understand. Bernie, how well do you know my client?"

"After eight or so years, I think very well in the context of his association with our Boys and Girls Club," I began.

"Could you share some of your insights with me, please?"

"Well, Larry, Camino knows right from wrong. He gets on well with members and staff and has a real interest in participating with our disabled members. Our friend is a high school dropout, at grade ten, I think. On the few occasions Camino or his younger brother have gotten into trouble at the clubhouse that were serious enough for us to need to contact their parents, we would run into a communication problem. You see, neither parent can speak English or French." I took a deep breath. "Larry, your client has very few friends, if any. He is easily led and has difficulty asserting himself with his peer group. Do you know that Camino is a loner, who is very sorry for what has happened? The bottom line is, Larry, I see no good being achieved by putting this young man in jail," I concluded.

"I see. What alternatives do you suggest, Bernie?" the lawyer inquired.

"Well, a term of probation with a strict community service provision is required. To this end, the Boys and Girls Club would be prepared to provide both counselling and supervision of any Community Service Order, say up to three times per week. He should be restricted from running with known troublemakers and be required to hold a full-time job or return to school full time. If he chooses to go to school, the Boys and Girls Club will provide him with homework and tutorial support. That's about it, Larry."

"Wow. Could you put all that in writing and get it to me today?" was the lawyer's unexpected response.

"That's not necessary, Larry. I have told Camino that, subject to your approval, I would be willing to be in court tomorrow."

"It would be very helpful if you could attend court tomorrow. My problem is that there is a "pre-sentence report" that has very few of the insights you have just provided. We need your comments in writing. They will be distributed to the judge and the Crown, prior to tomorrow's appearance. Can you possibly do it, Bernie?" he pleaded.

"Sure. How about I try to get it to you by two p.m. today?"

"Fine!" was his one-word response.

It was at this point that I remembered Camino. He was hanging on my every word. I became somewhat self-conscious about having talked so freely about someone who was sitting right in front of me.

"How many copies do you require, Larry?" I asked, as I changed my focus back to the telephone.

"Don't worry about that. We will look after it here. Look forward to receiving your letter at two p.m. today. Thanks."

"You're welcome. By the way Larry, Camino nearly screwed up. I was tempted, for a moment, not to telephone you," I said, looking directly at Camino.

The young man flinched.

"My God. What did he do?" the lawyer shouted unexpectedly into the telephone. He was so loud that his client, across the table from me, could hear the question.

"You tell your lawyer how you nearly screwed up by being late this morning." I demanded, as I thrust the telephone into Camino's hand. Of course I could hear only Camino's side of the conversation but I could guess the rest.

"Hi . . . Yes . . . I got here late . . . to his office . . . I know, he told me already . . . Sure, here he is . . . I'll do that!"

Throughout this exchange over the telephone, Camino and I maintained eye contact.

"I'm sorry, Bernie," Camino said with a deep sigh, as he handed the telephone back to me.

"Hi, Larry. Besides telling Camino not to be late getting to court tomorrow, I will offer him some advice on dress. Okay?"

"How will he get there?"

I placed a hand over the mouthpiece. "Your lawyer wants to know how you will get to court."

"Walk, of course!" the young man replied.

"Walking, Larry," I relayed.

"I don't like the sound of that, Bernie."

"Nor do I. Leave that to Camino and me to figure out. In the meantime, I had better get on with that letter."

"Thanks very much, Bernie. Camino is most fortunate to be a member of the Boys and Girls Club and to have someone like you on his side," the lawyer replied.

"That's okay. After all, Camino is one of my boys," I said, with a tilt of the head and a smile for a clearly relieved young man.

Tuesday, 9:20 a.m.

"Hello, Bernie. Am I on time?" was Camino's greeting.

"Good grief, you are ten minutes early. How do you feel today?"

"Okay, thanks. Bernie, did you get that letter to Mr. Rossey?" he asked.

"Sure did. You look smart in that sweater. Quite acceptable."

"Thanks. I got this sweater a couple of Christmases ago from my aunt. This the first time I am wearing it," he said, softly to himself.

Well, to keep a long story short, Camino and I arrived at the appointed courtroom fifteen minutes early.

Ten-thirty a.m. came and went and no sign of Mr. Rossey or any action in the courtroom.

The time passed very slowly. Camino became extremely tense. His left leg visibly shook as he wrung his hands repeatedly.

At 10:40 a.m. the lawyer appeared with his black robes flapping behind him, like bat's wings. Following greetings, he took his young client aside for a brief consultation. Both men then returned to where I was seated.

"Sorry to be late, Bernie. You should know that the Crown is somewhat sceptical about your letter. He wants to review it with his officials. He also reserves the right to cross-examine you. Consequently, the case has been deferred until 2:30 p.m. this afternoon. I do hope you can stay," the lawyer explained.

"Well, I had planned to get away by noon. I have a dinner appointment in Whitby, near Toronto, this evening. Getting out of Ottawa any later than noon will screw all that up."

"I know, Bernie."

"Larry, is that letter not good enough?" Camino, loudly clearing his throat, interrupted my question, to the lawyer.

Looking in his direction I observed a dry-lipped, ashen-faced, frightened young man whose Adam's apple was dancing up and down.

Raising my eyebrows and letting out a deep breath, my right hand motioned Camino to come over to me. "Well, my young friend, I guess you will have to put up with me for the rest of this morning and most of the afternoon. Okay?" I patted his shoulder.

"Sure, Bernie." His right hand brushed his eyes.

Mr. Rossey said, "That's great, Bernie. I will meet both of you here at, let's say, 2:10 or 2:15 p.m. Okay, Camino?"

"Oh, yes. We will be here," the client assured his lawyer. Mr. Rossey departed, enveloped in his flowing black legal robes.

Needless to say, all the parties showed up and entered the courtroom on time. The previous trial had resumed following the lunch break. Camino and I sat in the public gallery.

At about 3:05 p.m., the presiding judge excused himself with the phrase, "The court will recess for ten minutes." Everyone stood up and the judge departed.

As we sat down, a hubbub filled the courtroom. My companion added to its level, with the question, "Where does he play?"

"What?" I asked, somewhat bemused by the question.

"Where does that guy, the judge, play?" my companion asked, in all seriousness.

"Why on earth would you ask such a question?"

"Well at school, we *play* at recess."

"No, Camino. The judge has gone to his chamber or office to consult some law books. He probably wanted to look up a point of law in order to end the trial. So when they stop or adjourn the activities in a court, it is referred to as a 'recess.' Do you understand?"

"Not really. But that's okay," the young man assured me. I shook my head in disbelief.

It must have been about 3:25 p.m. when finally the oath was administered to me while I stood in the witness box.

"Tell us your name?"

"Bernard J. Muzeen."

"How do you spell it?" intoned the court clerk.

"M-u-z-e-e-n," I responded firmly.

"Thank you, Mr. Muzeen. Could you please tell the court your present position and place of employment?" asked Camino's lawyer.

"I am presently the executive director and general manager of the Boys and Girls Club of Ottawa–Carleton. I have been in the employment of that organization since 1970."

"Mr. Muzeen. Do you know the defendant, and if so, under what circumstances?"

"I have known Camino—I mean the defendant—for about eight years, as a member, teen leader and volunteer at the Centre Town Clubhouse of the Boys and Girls Club."

"Over that period of time have you been able to form an opinion about this individual, Mr. Muzeen?"

"Yes, sir. Camino tends to be an introspective loner who has few friends. He is co-operative with, and respectful of, the Club staff. Camino knows right from wrong. As a teen leader, he has developed an interest in our Disabled Children's Program. He continues this interest as a community volunteer, now that he is over eighteen years of age."

"Mr. Muzeen, does the Boys and Girls Club have the ability to provide supervision for someone who is assigned to undertake a Community Service Order?"

"Yes, sir."

"How would this be undertaken, and has the Club experience in this area?" The lawyer flipped the sleeves of his robe, with a dramatic gesture.

"Yes, sir. Presently the Boys and Girls Club provides Community Service Order supervision in co-operation with the Family Court and Adult Probation Service. I would like to add that the Boys and Girls Club has the ability to provide guidance and counselling services to children and youth, without their necessarily being in conflict with the law."

"Thank you, Mr. Muzeen. Knowing my client as you have attested, have you formed an opinion as to how this situation might be addressed?"

"Well, sir, I can assure you that he is sorry. However, he does not seem to understand the seriousness of these charges. I feel no good would be served by sending Camino to jail. I envision a term of Probation and Community Service Order. To this end, the Boys and Girls Club would be prepared to provide for a Community Service Order placement, for up to three times per week. These and other points were provided to you in a letter."

"Thank you, Mr. Muzeen," Mr. Rossey said as he resumed his seat.

"Mr. Muzeen. You are aware of the reporting requirements for Community Service Orders?" the Crown asked.

"Yes, sir."

"Would you be able to act accordingly, should the court place Camino B. on probation with a Community Service Order placement at the Boys and Girls Club?"

"Let me assure the court, that should Camino be placed at the Boys and Girls Club on a Community Service Order, and were he to fail to fulfill its terms, I would report him to the court through the proper channels. Sir, you should know that we have had to take such action in the past. I can assure you that it will continue, on an as needed basis, in the future."

"I see. Mr. Muzeen. You said—er, you said—excuse me," the Crown said, as he thumbed through the papers on the table in front of him.

"Ah yes," he said, holding a sheet of paper in his hand. I think it was a copy of my letter.

"Mr. Muzeen, you state that the defendant does not understand the seriousness of the charges. Could you explain what you mean to the court?"

"Maybe the word 'understanding' is inappropriate." I shifted my weight from one foot to the other. "'Comprehension' is more descriptive. I believe that it is a question of comprehension. May I give Your Honour an example?" I asked the judge, as I looked into his steel-grey eyes.

The judge, dressed in black robes with a red stole, nodded his head in assent.

He turned his throne-like chair in my direction.

"Sir, I truly believe that this young man does not comprehend the nature of the charges brought against him. Something happened a few minutes ago that may underscore this point." I took a deep breath to clear my head and to keep my cool.

"Sir, Camino and I attended the previous trial. Your Honour, do you recall that during the previous trial you called a recess?"

The judge inclined his head.

"Well, sir, after the court recessed, Camino turned to me and in all seriousness asked, 'Where does he play?' You see, your Honour, Camino equates your recess with those he enjoyed at school. That is an example of what I mean when I say that it is really 'a question of comprehension.' I believe this young man does not understand the seriousness of the charges, Your Honour."

There was a period of silence. It was broken when the judge's high-backed chair was swivelled to face the court.

Looking back at my questioner, I noticed that he was seated.

Camino was sentenced to a term of probation with a Community Service Order at the Boys and Girls Club.

* * *

With the passage of time, this young man provided many hours of support services that enriched and expanded the lives of some seriously disabled children. Through it, his self-confidence grew and he talked about upgrading his education.

During my most recent contact with Camino, some five years after this occurrence, he was still talking about improving his level of education. Sad to say, there has been no action on his behalf.

Oh well, you can't win them all.

Commentary:

Coincidence plays a great part in life. Look at the series of them in this case:

- Correcting the midyear computer budget error in the office rather than at home.
- Camino's decision to walk past the clubhouse after work on the chance that I would be there.
- His almost shaking the doors off their hinges (I would not have heard him otherwise).
- His lawyer being an alumnus of the Boys and Girls Club.
- The calling of a recess during the previous trial.
- The final coincidence that there was a Boys and Girls Club in place to serve the children and youth throughout the Ottawa–Carleton Community.

ALTERNATIVE WORDING

One of the most frequent problems institutions such as a Boys and Girls Club, school, summer camp, and sports organizations face is assisting young people in finding and using socially acceptable wording in moments of frustration.

These words, which tend to begin with "B," "S," "F," "J," and "D," are all unacceptable and can be injurious.

The challenge is to have youngsters stop and consider the negative impact that such verbal abuse has on others as well as on themselves.

There are ways to deal with such situations. These include developing a heightened sensitivity towards the sensibilities of others; providing actual opportunities to attain better verbal skills; refusing to tolerate or offer verbal abuse, while offering examples that demonstrate better communication skills; and creating an environment in which those who "miss-speak" are provided an opportunity to learn, accept and be introduced to an alternative vocabulary.

Skateboarders, football players, tennis players, swimmers and other athletes tend to be victims of their own verbal abuse. This results in a devaluation of many of their outstanding achievements. This verbal abuse can also have a devastating impact on coaches, teammates and officials.

Besides an immediate loss of focus on the challenge at hand, there is a loss of energy, determination and objectivity that will have to be rebuilt. Those sportsmen who redirect their energies in a positive manner tend to accomplish and surpass their goals on a consistent basis. They learn quickly that verbal abuse directed at hockey pucks, tennis balls, teammates, skateboards, officials or the facilities accomplishes very little.

Swearing at teammates, opponents and/or officials tends to indicate that the athlete's limit has been reached. At this point, a timeout is required, to preserve gains.

The challenge for the coach is to obtain a measure of the physical and emotional capacity of each athlete, in order to be able to anticipate such outbursts. Timely withdrawal can lessen negative behaviour and retain gains. In this way, the threshold of positive accomplishment can be increased.

The requirement of a positive mental attitude and the ability to visualize the successful outcome of the athletic challenge, be it trampoline, fencing, skateboarding, archery, diving, or other individual sports, has been demonstrated repeatedly. Sport teams that can attain single-mindedness and a common focus have the seed of success that will blossom as skills are acquired.

The following are examples of circumstances that provided those "teachable moments" that have arisen, from time to time.

GARBAGE MOUTH

"Now, you sit right there, and don't say anything, while I talk with Bernie," demanded the physical education director as he stood in the doorway of my office.

"Oh, sure!" responded a child who was out of my line of vision.

"What's up, Dave? Who have you got out there?"

"It's Jerry. Bernie, we've got to do something about his 'garbage mouth' before someone kills him. I've had it!" my exasperated co-worker advised. "By the way, here's his membership card." He cast a blue card on the worktable. It indicated we were dealing with a junior-age Club member. A quick review of the membership register indicated that Jerry was a relatively new member.

"Now calm down and tell me what happened," I responded softly.

Pulling a red leather-covered chair out from the worktable Dave dropped onto it rather heavily and took several deep breaths. "Jerry uses foul language and it is constant. It almost got him beaten up by a couple of very angry senior members. After I made them back off from Jerry, the only thanks I got was a mouthful of verbal abuse which he screamed at the top of his voice."

"What do you think we should do about Jerry's bad language?" I said, raising my voice so that the unseen child could hear the question.

"I don't know." Dave stole a glance towards the open door. "One thing that will not work is talking to him. The Lord knows I've tried. Jerry straightens out for a short time then reverts back to the 'garbage mouth' all over again." Dave stood up and left the office.

I allowed about ten minutes to elapse following Dave's departure, to provide Jerry a chance to calm down. As those minutes passed I became aware of a steady thudding, emanating from outside my office.

"If you don't want to sit there for the rest of the day stop that noise immediately!" I thundered.

Quiet descended instantly—so much so that I could detect a muffled whistle blast from the distant gymnasium.

Eventually I stepped out of my office. Sitting in an oversize chair was Jerry. He was of slight build, with large brown eyes, and a round blemish-free face that gave him a cherub-like appearance.

"Hi, Bernie," he said weakly as he looked up at me.

Shrugging my shoulders, I folded my arms across my chest and leaned against the doorframe without responding.

When his attempted smile produced no reaction from me the boy cast his gaze to the floor. It soon became apparent through his hand motions, and the soundless movement of lips, that he was debating internally his response to this predicament.

Sliding down the doorframe I sat on the floor so that I was at eye level with Jerry. "Did you hear what Dave told me, Jerry?" I asked.

He nodded his head affirmatively, without looking in my direction.

"We—you and I—are going to have to deal with this today. Here and now. Do you understand?"

An affirmative nodding of the boy's head ended with his face buried in his hands. A few minutes later he stood up and walked over to where I was sitting, wiping tears from his flushed cheeks with the back of his hands.

"I'm sorry." He rested one hand gently on my shoulder.

"Jerry, I'm not the one you offended today." I stood up.

Re-entering my office, I picked up his membership card. Jerry extended his right hand, palm up, in a non-verbal request for its return.

"I'm not sure you deserve it back. You do know that without a card you cannot come here?" I tapped it on my chin to underscore my point.

"Oh, Bernie! Please . . . I don't have anywhere . . ." his voice trailed off as tears ran down his cheeks at the thought of losing his access to the Boys and Girls Club.

"Is it okay for me to invite Dave in here so you can straighten it out with him?" I picked up the intercom as I spoke.

The boy nodded his assent.

Dave arrived a few minutes later.

"I'm sorry, Dave. Really!" Jerry thrusted his right hand in Dave's direction.

"Jerry, you verbally abuse other members, volunteers, and me. I am not so sure that you mean it when you say 'sorry' this time." Dave commented, softly grasping the boy's hand.

"I really do . . . don't I, Bernie?" said Jerry, turning a pleading face in my direction.

"Yes, I do believe you, Jerry."

"Fine. But Jerry is banned from the gym for the rest of today. In that way we can keep him safe from the big guys getting back at him when I'm not looking."

"Sounds like a wise move," I assured him as he headed back to his duties. "The next time Jerry comes to the gymnasium we will all have a fresh start," he added.

"Jerry, you are one very lucky young man. Dave and the other staff want to protect you from the wrath of those you offend. So please stay away from the gym for the rest of today. Do you understand?"

He nodded his head in agreement.

"Jerry, are you a new member?"

"Yes. I joined last month."

"Have you been told not to swear?"

"Yeah. They kicked me out of the swimming pool and the games room, for that!" He tilted his head and smiled.

"And still you have not gotten the message, have you?"

"What do you mean?"

"You understand that we all have to get along with each other. That means that you must respect yourself . . . others . . . and the Club, in that order. Your 'garbage mouth,' as Dave calls it, would indicate that you have little or no self-respect."

He looked at me wide mouthed.

"Jerry, if you can't respect yourself how on earth do you expect to have others respect you, or to want to have you as a friend?"

The boy licked his lips.

"Do you have any friends at the Club . . . at school . . . or in your neighbourhood?"

To each point the little boy shook "no" with his head. "I don't mean to swear. It just comes out when I think someone is mad at me or is going to hit me." Jerry seemed to be talking to himself.

"The next time you verbally abuse my staff I will telephone your mother."

"No—you wouldn't!" he exclaimed with an impish smile.

Picking up the telephone I dialled his home number. The phone rang four times.

"Hello?" It was a female voice.

A look of horror swept across my young companion's face as he recognized his mother's voice. Tears, which he attempted to check by rubbing his eyes with the back of his hand, started to flow once more.

"Hello? Hello . . . is anyone there?"

We heard the click of a telephone receiver being hung up.

"Jerry, what was the lesson you just learned?" I whispered.

"Not to swear, sir!"

"No. Wrong," was my immediate reply.

"I don't understand. You want me to stop swearing, don't you?"

"Of course I do. Jerry, a few minutes ago I said that I would telephone your mother. Is that correct?"

"Yeah."

"Did I telephone her?"

"Yeah."

"I beg your pardon. 'Yeah.' What's that supposed to mean?"

"Sorry. I mean yes, Bernie. Er—sir." He smiled.

"Bernie it is." I smiled. "Now, Jerry, what was the message I was trying to communicate to you?"

"I don't know."

"My friend, please understand that when I say I will do something, such as calling your mother, I will do it. Understand now? "

"Oh yeah . . . I mean yes." We exchanged smiles.

"Do you want this?" I waved his membership card in the air.

"Yes, please."

"Let's you and I understand one thing. If you persist in swearing then I will invite your mother to come to this office and you will have to tell her all the swear words you say at our Club. Do you now believe me, young man?"

"Now I believe you." He let out a great sigh of relief while stealing a quick glance in the direction of the telephone.

"Besides telephoning your mother I have all kinds of interesting ways to help you overcome your bad habit of swearing. Would you like to learn what they are?"

"No, thanks!" he shouted.

"Get out of here and co-operate with my staff. Before long you will make lots of friends. Just put a stop to the swearing."

"Thanks, Bernie," Jerry said as I handed him his membership card.

"Sorry, Bernie," he said, as he paused and turned at the door to my office, before heading back to activities in the clubhouse.

"Say *sorry* to yourself when you next pass a mirror. Because you hurt yourself every time you swear, Jerry. It all starts and ends with you being true to yourself," I concluded.

Commentary:

Verbal abuse often indicates:

- A lack of self-respect
- A sense of insecurity
- Fear
- Loneliness
- Internal rage
- A call for attention

Swearing affirms an inability to fit in, in social settings such as a peer group, team, gang, club, school and so on.

Leaders need to be aware that such antisocial behaviour has a self-destructive component.

Swearing is often:

- An act of rebellion
- Rejection of social situations
- Intention to harm others
- A cry for help

Jerry, with great effort and understanding, was able to break a very bad habit. He went on to become a valued Club member over an eight-year period.

LOCKER ROOM TALK

A group of preteens were sitting in the locker room. Their conversation was so loud that it could be overheard in the adjoining check-in/check-out area without their realizing it.

I was in that area checking the stock of towels and swim shorts.

Their conversation was saturated with foul phrases. Enough being enough, I entered the locker room.

"Hold it just there. Do you know the meaning of all of those words you guys are using?" I demanded.

"No." "Not really." "Some," were the mixed responses from the boys. Several smiled, while Billy laughed aloud.

"It's not funny. Why on earth are you using those words? Do you really know what they mean?" I challenged the eleven- and twelve-year-olds.

"Well, everyone uses them," Billy shot back.

"I beg your pardon. Everyone? Billy, you say everyone uses these words. When did I use them or when did our lifeguard use any of them to you or other Club members? Have you heard the front desk clerk say them? Or maybe the gamesroom supervisor? Eh, fellows?" I pressed.

"No, none of them," Mark said softly.

"How about the police?"

Their heads shook no in unison.

"Obviously, it must be your teachers or the school principal—maybe they use those words in your presence?"

"No," Billy sighed.

"Hang on a moment, guys. Didn't Billy just say that everyone uses these words?"

"Well, he meant *almost* everybody," Steve explained.

"Okay, I will accept that. Guys, what would happen if you used any of those words at home?"

"My mother would kill me," Steve said.

"I would be grounded," said Mark.

"I just don't use them," interjected another boy.

"Now hold it, fellows. Let me understand the situation. None of you are allowed to use these words at home, or in the presence of your mothers or fathers. Am I correct?"

Heads nodded in unison once more.

"But you have the nerve to use them here at the Club, and in front of other children. That is a heck of a double standard. I think it is a matter we should share with your parents!"

"Bernie, no, please!" "Oh, God." "I'm dead," were examples of their emotional responses to my recommendation.

Steve summed up the reaction of his friends. "Sorry. We were just talking among ourselves."

"Look, guys. By using these words at home, on the street, at school, here at the Club, or among yourselves indicates a lack of respect."

No one responded.

"Do you like each other?" I swept my hand through the air as I pointed to each boy.

"Sure do." "Yeah." "Guess so," was their mixed response.

"Then don't insult each other or your own intelligence by using such disgusting and unacceptable words to each other. Good God, you are all friends! I would hate to be around to hear what any of you would say if you were angry!" I arched my eyebrows in mock horror.

There was a collective giggle.

"Now, children," I continued in a mocking tone, "do I need to telephone each of your mummies or daddies or have you learned your lesson for today?"

"We understand," Billy said, while his friends indicated their agreement.

"The next time you fellows wish to engage in locker room talk, try words like "fig," "fudge," "spud," or "heck." At this point all the youngsters smiled broadly.

My message had been received, understood, and I hope accepted.

Commentary:

Encouraging teenagers and others to be true to themselves and the values of their families has proven to be a powerful tool in helping resolve the problem of antisocial language.

THE SOAP TREATMENT

"Bernie. Peter used that word again," a wide-eyed seven-year-old reported.

"What did you do to make him say it?" was my reaction.

"Nothing. Honest, Bernie."

"Where was he when he used it?"

"In the gym," said the boy, as he pointed in that direction.

"Then go and tell David—he's the guy in charge—if Peter uses it again," I advised.

I was interested in completing the paperwork necessary to ensure the orderly operation of our summer camp, Camp Minwassin: the budgets, food services contracts, appointment of a nurse, maintenance list, and the text of the annual appeal letter.

My concentration on the paperwork was again broken abruptly, this time by the sound of David's voice.

"Can you do something with this guy's bad mouth? He just will not listen to me," he almost shouted, while glaring at his young escort.

I looked up to see that Peter was the object of his comment.

Peter, a seven-year-old, was surrounded by a cluster of boys of the same age group. Some seemed to delight in the predicament this boy faced.

"What did you say, Peter?" I demanded.

The boys, with Peter, burst into repressed giggling.

The object of my attention rolled his large brown eyes from side to side in response to their outburst. Setting them on me, he shrugged his shoulders in a wordless gesture.

"It's the worst swear word you can think of, Bernie," David interjected.

An arched eyebrow was Peter's only reaction.

"We are going to have to deal with this. You know that, Peter?" I said sternly, as I cast my eyes across his impressionable escort.

At this point I left the office and went to the shower room. I searched for the largest bar of wet, slimy soap and returned with it to the office.

Peter's eyes were transfixed on the soap in my hand. As tears brimmed up in his large brown eyes, I cleared the young escorts out of my office. David returned to his duties in the gymnasium.

"Put this soap between your fingers and thumb," I directed.

Gingerly, Peter took the soap. Once he had it securely held between his fingers and thumb, he set his imploring eyes on me.

"Now, my young friend, you just sit there and concentrate on that bar of soap. In a few minutes I will take a break from all this paperwork. At that time, you had better let me know what that slimy bar of soap could be used for. Do you understand?"

A nod of the head was the boy's wordless response.

I returned to the paperwork, while giving an occasional glance at my young companion. He seemed to be totally absorbed in the task assigned. Peter never removed his eyes from the bar of soap.

After about ten minutes or so, we had the following encounter.

"Peter, can you tell me to what uses that soap could be put to?"

Turning his tearstained face to me, his head nodded affirmatively.

"Then tell me?"

"Wash my mouth!" A wave of tears ran down his cheeks.

"Oh dear, oh dear. I thought that soap was used to wash your face, hands, hair, feet, maybe even your ears and neck. But do you know, Peter, you have just made a new suggestion as how we can use a bar of soap."

Peter pressed his lips tight as he shook his head.

"Remember young fellow, the next time you swear, that it was your suggestion that we use soap to wash out a mouth. Right, Peter?"

After a few moments of silent reflection, a smile enveloped Peter's face. He realized he was off the hook. This time.

"Do we need to wash your mouth out this time?"

"Oh, no, Bernie," he smiled sweetly.

"No, thank you!" I reminded him.

"No thank you, Bernie," Peter responded, moving to the edge of the large red leather chair, in anticipation that this ordeal was just about complete.

"What have you learned today, Peter?"

"Not to swear."

"Why?"

"Because I will get my mouth washed out?" he question, with eyebrows arched.

"No . . . no, my young friend, that is not the real reason," I said, somewhat exasperated. "Peter, the real reason why you should not swear is that you will not have friends. You can hurt people when you swear at them. Other guys will not play with you, as swearing upsets them. Does that make sense to you?"

The boy nodded his head in the affirmative.

"Peter, would your parents be proud of you because you can swear?"

"No," he shook his head.

"I think those are the real lessons for today. I am sure that the guys that brought you in here, with David, would like to be your friends. But if you swear at them, when you make a mistake, it could upset them. Do you really understand that, Peter?"

"Yeah," he let out a great sigh.

"I beg your pardon?" I scowled.

"Oh, uh, yes, Bernie," he smiled.

"Now Peter, you are going to have to use that soap, right now," I informed him.

He let out an audible gasp. Peter fixed me with unblinking eyes and an incredulous expression on his face.

I smiled broadly. "Get out of here and wash your face. Then come back and see me when you are finished. Okay, Peter?" I asked, with a smile.

"Okay, Bernie. I will be right back," he replied, as he scampered out of my office.

For my part, I went to the gym and invited the group that had escorted Peter previously to return to my office.

"What did you do?" "Did you use the soap?" "Where is Peter?" "Did you kick him out of the Club?" are examples of the questions they threw at me as we walked back to my office.

"Okay, guys. Settle down," I said on arriving at the office.

"Peter and I have come to an understanding. I will get cross with any of you who teases him so that he gets so mad he forgets our agreement. Do you all understand?" I wagged my index finger, in their direction.

A collective "Yeah," filled the air.

"He's an okay guy, just like you fellows." At this moment Peter entered the office. His friends turned in his direction.

"We understand each other, eh Peter?" I asked, with a wink.

"Sure do, Bernie!" he looked around at the other boys.

"Had to use the soap today, eh?" I said, in a matter of fact tone.

"I guess so," he replied, dropping his head, so that the others could not see the smile on his face.

His friends let out a collective gasp. Eyes popped. Several moved away from me.

"Peter, these guys have all promised not to get you so mad that you have to swear. Right, guys?"

"Sure thing!" "Right on!" "Okay," were the replies.

There were smiles and high fives all around.

"Now get out of here. I have all this work to do." I returned to my desk, the children to the gymnasium.

About ten minutes had elapsed before I was again interrupted by a gentle knock on the office door. "Bernie, can I ask you something, but I don't want you to get mad with me?" asked David, with a scowl on his face, as he half closed my office door.

"Sure, what is it?" I asked, pointing to a chair, for him to sit down.

"Did you use the 'soap treatment' on Peter?" he asked in a hoarse whisper.

"No," was my shocked, one word reply.

"That's not what he is telling the other kids. Peter is saying that the soap was used. He also boasts that it did not hurt."

Good for Peter . . . he had found a creative way to be the centre of his friends' attention without swearing—albeit at my expense!

Commentary:

The threat of the "soap treatment" has worked repeatedly for over forty years, without ever actually having to be administered as suggested by Peter.

IT'S IN THE BOOK

Twelve- to fifteen-year-olds seem to use obnoxious and crude language as their "rite of passage." To simply demand that they conform to acceptable community standards that have little or no consequences to their values or lifestyle is as effective as a ram butting away at a dam wall.

Whether talking among themselves or to others, their speech is flavoured with foul words that have several objectives:

- Deliver shock value
- Show contempt
- Display anger
- Cause offence
- Provoke a response in kind

This approach to communication reflects a limited education, betrays ignorance that these remarks can be hurtful, and amount to no more than insensitive "bafflegab." Ninety per cent of this unacceptable chatter and/or foul language falls into this last category.

The antidote is to challenge these youth to question their values. This can be accomplished through self-discovery, family standards, education and retribution. Invariably, I find that family standards and practices along with group expectations is a good point of departure in addressing this concern. Those adults who have attempted retaliation in kind have found that it does not resolve this problem.

In over forty years of working with children and youth, I have found that the provision of an alternative vocabulary can provide a long-lasting and positive effect.

The following is an example of one approach that I found to be effective on several occasions. It involves fourteen-year-old Jack. He was considered to be a tough nut. With time and perseverance he was able to modify his language.

* * *

"Jack. Am I to believe that you do not understand the meaning of some of those words you just used to insult several Club members?" I asked, more in sorrow than in anger.

"Oh sure. I know their meaning," he sneered.

"Then you would know that they are clearly out of place and totally unacceptable here. You are really showing your ignorance to everyone by using inappropriate words. Because in many cases they have no relevance to the particular situation you are seeking to address," I explained.

"So?" Jack leaned back so that his chair stood on its rear legs. His eyes were fixed on a model train displayed on the credenza in my office.

"It seems to me that what you and I need is to learn some alternative and socially acceptable words. Don't you agree?"

Jack mouthed an unspoken swear word.

"*I beg your pardon!*" I responded, slamming the flat of my hand on the worktable that stood between us. Its explosive tone brought Jack's undivided attention back to me.

"I guess so," Jack responded, after he recovered from the shock of my action.

His eyes now locked with mine. If looks could kill I would have been struck dead.

"Good. You see that red book over there?" I gestured to the bookshelf that stood to the left of the office window.

"Which one?" he asked

"The red one with the gold letters. Second from the left."

"Oh yeah."

"It is a dictionary. It has thirty-seven pages of words beginning with the letter 'F.' The next time you are brought to my attention for using bad language, we will sit down and look up six to ten words, all of which begin with the letter 'F,' or 'S,' or 'B' that are socially acceptable."

"How come?" he sneered.

"So that you can better handle situations when you are at a loss for words—when you are angry and frustrated at someone," I explained.

A weak smile crossed his face. "Come on, Bernie. You wouldn't do that to me. Would you?" he asked, as he leaned forward.

"Just go out there and swear. Then you will see what I will do. Not only would we look up words. You will have to read their meanings back to me," I said, with all the authority I could muster.

Jack nodded his head slowly.

"And should you repeat any of those cuss words after that, you will be required to write out the meaning of each new word we learn from that dictionary. Believe me, my friend," I added, as I leaned close to Jack.

"I believe you. I believe that you would try something like that, Bernie. But some of these words come out, before I know it," Jack explained breathlessly, his face flushed.

"My friend, there is always an answer. Whenever you are at a loss for words you will find it is 'in the book.' That big red book," I offered with a smile. "However, the best and most effective answer rests with you, by saying nothing. Jack, you are the only one who can control your brain and mouth when they want you to spit out swear words."

"I know. I know. But I can't help it. They just come out," Jack said, more to himself than to me.

"Okay, buddy. If or when that happens, quickly apologize or say something like, 'Oops, where did that come from?' or maybe, 'Did I say that? Sorry.' People will realize that you did not mean to offend, and will credit you for trying to control yourself."

Jack nodded his head in silent agreement.

"It may also prevent the confrontations and fights that seem to bring you to my attention from starting. Jack, you and only you control what comes out of your mouth."

Getting up, I walked over to the bookshelf and selected the dictionary. Dropping it on the table in front of Jack, I asked, "Do we need to look up a couple of words, now?"

"No way, Bernie. I'm out of here," he replied, as he pushed the book away. "I don't need to look up anything right now," was his parting remark.

Two or three weeks after this encounter Jack was back in my office for swearing.

When I placed the red and gold dictionary on the table, Jack responded, "Oh, come on, Bernie. I thought you were kidding." Shaking his head, he added, "God, I should have known better."

Jack and I proceeded to look up several acceptable words.

To his credit Jack learned to modulate his language by the time he was in grade ten.

Jack went on to secure a job in the record section of a major chain store.

Commentary:

- In thirty years, no Boys and Girls Club member has pushed me to carry out the second step of this exercise—to write out the meaning of each acceptable word.

- I generally found that once youth have been alerted to the fact that their offensive language is unacceptable, that it is not cool, that they are going to be ostracized, they do make a real effort to change their use of offensive language. Motivated by ego, self-preservation and status, youngsters will begrudgingly modify the level and use of abusive language.

- It is not very often that I have come across young people who do not give a care about their self-image.

PROMISES MADE / PROMISES KEPT

During their formative years young people make what they believe to be solemn promises. Many of these promises or pledges are made in an attempt to be true to self and each other. The purposes and practice of making such undertakings seem to fade as the individual advances in age and life experience.

A promise made and a promise kept can be regarded as a test of goodwill, purpose, stamina, discipline and vision for themselves, their friends, their loved ones, their peers, their coaches and leaders, and their community.

To fail to fulfill these undertakings can have serious negative effects on those of tender years.

From time to time adults extract promises from children and expect them to be kept. These same adults all too often make and fail to keep *their* promises to these same youngsters, with abandon. It is little wonder that by the time children reach their teen years they have generally become cynical about the whole process of making and keeping promises.

This could be the root of the attitude of mistrust between the generations. I am convinced, after forty years of working with children and youth, that the negative attitude between the generations is seen as a form of self-protection. It is a guard against the hurt and disappointment caused by unkept promises.

Adults tend to dismiss the process of "promise making and promise keeping" as just another phase in young people's lives. Some show intolerance when a child accomplishes or fulfils a promise. Others make excuses that the accomplishment does not measure up to the adults' expectations.

On balance, promises made by children during their formative years tend to be cherished and binding for many years into the future.

In order for a promise to be made and kept, both parties to the process must be alive to the significance of failure for either party.

The dividends of "promises kept" are positive: they are joyful, life changing, real, and memorable; and they offer hope. The following stories provide insights into the processes of "a promise made/a promise kept."

The Best Man

Dane was a good basketball player, in spite of the fact that his opponents towered head and shoulders over him. His assertive leadership and sense of confidence with his peers may have resulted from the fact that he was the oldest of four brothers.

This teenager was a good student. He mirrored his father's drive, confidence and business acumen. Furthermore, he showed sensitivity towards others, with a mature insight that reflected Dane's close relationship with his grandfather.

Dane was stimulated by, and rose to the challenge of, leadership at the Boys Club, his high school, and sports teams. This young man held great promise for the future due to the benefits of positive role models and the promises they kept during his formative years.

One day, we were sitting around and talking about what we would be doing in five and ten years. Dane was seventeen years of age at that time. He had a clear vision of what the future held. He laid out a plan of action that included graduating from high school and university, becoming a teacher, getting married, and continuing our friendship.

As for myself, I made a number of undertakings. They included becoming a Boys Club director, taking university courses, camping during the summer, tracing my family heritage in England, and remaining friends with Dane.

Dane pointed out that I had not included marriage. There was some good-natured ribbing as to who would marry either of us.

"Whether you get married or not, Bernie, I will make you this promise. You will be the best man at my wedding. I mean it. You wait and see," he said solemnly.

"Get off it, Dane. You have to consider one of your brothers. If not, you may prefer to have a high school or university friend, not me!" I countered.

"I told you. It's a promise I wish to make to you," he stated firmly.

"I don't know what to say, but thanks. Sure, I would be glad and honoured to be your best man," I responded.

"Agreed," he said, extending his right hand. A firm handshake sealed this heartfelt promise.

The years passed. Our respective hometowns changed. We were able to follow, with keen interest, each other's accomplishments.

So it was that many years later I had settled in Ottawa as the executive director/general manager of the Boys and Girls Club.

Dane had become a physical education teacher and department head of a high school.

Dane telephoned me on a cold winter evening. After an exchange of greetings and update of each other's activities, he cut in with the question, "Do you remember the promise we made when you worked at the Oshawa Boys Club?"

"We made a lot of them to each other, in those days," was my reply, somewhat puzzled by his question.

"No. I mean the promise I made you, should I get married?"

"I sure do. I would be delighted to be your best man. Also remember that you have to be mine," I laughed.

"Sure will," he said happily.

We then spent some time talking about his bride, dates, reception, dress code and other details.

The experience of a promise fulfilled brought both of us great joy. It also reinforced the bonds of friendship and mutual respect, the foundation of which were laid so many years earlier.

This promise made and kept served like a bridge of trust and respect that spanned the years, and will last the both of us a lifetime.

The Telephone Call

"I don't care," said the defiant nine-year-old boy to me, as he folded his arms across his chest and slumped in the red leather chair next to my desk.

"But you must care, Pat," I countered. "You cannot disrupt the games of other Club members. How would you like it if I came along and spoiled a game you were playing?"

"I don't care. I could start the game all over again. I could start a new one. I don't care," he repeated, as if he was trying to reassure himself.

"What is your telephone number?" I asked.

"I don't know," he snapped.

"Come off it, Pat. You mean that a smart boy like you doesn't know his home telephone number? I am surprised," I stated with a touch of sarcasm.

"Patrick. My name is Patrick," the boy asserted, as he looked at me with narrowing eyes.

"Oh. I am sorry, Patrick. I find it difficult to believe that a boy your age does not know his home phone number. I can't believe that, not in this day and age." Picking up the intercom, I asked the front desk clerk to look up Patrick Lawrence's telephone number.

The boy in front of me motioned me to stop. When I turned my attention to him, he rattled off a phone number, which I jotted down.

A moment later the front desk clerk spoke. "Would you repeat that for me?" I said casually, before I hung up the intercom.

Comparing both telephone numbers, I turned to Patrick. "You do know your phone number. Well done," I responded, with a smile.

"Why do you need it?" the boy asked, as he shifted his weight in the oversized chair.

"Because I am going to talk to your mother."

"So?" was the boy's reaction.

"'So?' What do you mean, 'so'? It's you who doesn't care if you make other children unhappy by spoiling their games. It's you who doesn't care if I talk to your mother. It's you that is rude. It's you who has the attitude problem," was my response.

With a grim expression on my face and eyes fixed on my young companion, I picked up the telephone. Slowly, I dialled the first three digits. Then Patrick waved his hand to get my attention.

"Yes, what is it Patrick?" I asked, a touch of exasperation in my voice.

"What are you doing?" he asked, as he leaned forward.

"Telephoning your mother. But then that should not bother you because you don't care about that. Right, Patrick?"

"Why?"

"Because that was a promise I made to you, a few minutes ago."

"What are you going to tell her?" he inquired, as he held his right hand in the air.

Slowly I dialled the fourth number. The boy moved to the edge of his chair, waving his upraised hand. He had become somewhat agitated.

The fifth number was now dialled. Patrick was lightly pounding on the desk and repeating softly, "She will kill me. She will kill me." A tear rolled down his cheek.

The last two numbers were dialled in quick succession. The telephone was answered on the second ring.

"Good evening. Mrs. Lawrence, please?" I said, with eyes fixed on Patrick's tear-stained face.

"Yes."

"This is Bernie, at the Boys and Girls Club . . ." I took a deep breath.

Patrick had by now buried his face in his hands. His slight frame shook as he sobbed quietly.

"Have you any objection to Pat—I mean Patrick—taking part in archery lessons on Saturday?" I said, into the receiver.

"Are they safe and well supervised?"

"Oh yes, Mrs. Lawrence. They are strictly run and very safe. In fact it is an activity I supervise, these days," I assured her.

The boy's hands had slipped down to cover only his mouth and chin. His unblinking eyes settled on me.

"If he would like to, it's all right by me," his mother said.

"Good. He should be in the lower gym by 1:30 p.m. on Saturday."

"I hope Patrick is behaving himself."

By now Patrick's hands were clasped together just below his chin.

"No problem. Patrick's no problem. Good night and thank you, Mrs. Lawrence." I hung up.

Then Patrick and I looked at each other in silence for several moments.

"But you didn't say . . . I mean you didn't . . ." the child was at a loss for words, as he stuttered and pointed to the telephone.

"Look, young man. When I make a promise, you had better know that I keep it," I said, as I leaned forward to within inches of the boy's face.

"But you didn't say anything about me, Bernie," he stammered.

"I know. What was the promise I made to you a few minutes ago?"

"When?"

"Before I made that telephone call to your mother."

"You said you would tell her . . ." his eyes rolled in his head as if searching for the right answer.

"No, I said no such thing," I cut in. "What I told you was that I would talk to your mother. Yes or no?"

"Yes, you did."

"Did I talk to your mother?"

"Yes."

"Then that's it. Off you go." I gestured towards the office door.

Getting out of his chair, Patrick moved towards me. With his head tilted to the right the boy said in a conspiratorial tone, "But Bernie, you did not tell her what I did." He let out a great sigh.

"Oh, I forgot. Thanks for reminding me, Patrick. Now what did I do with your telephone number?" I playfully searched my desk for the telephone message pad.

"No, no, it's okay, Bernie. I promise not mess up other kid's games," Patrick assured me, as he rested his left hand on the phone.

"Patrick, when I promise to do something I will do it. You have seen that demonstrated today. I hope you understand."

He nodded his head.

"Have you just given me a promise, Patrick? Can I trust you to keep your promise?"

"You sure can, Bernie," he said, with a bright smile.

"Patrick, it seems fair to me that if you can call me Bernie I should be able to call you Pat. It can be seen as a sign of our friendship. What do you say?"

"Sounds okay to me, Bernie. When Mum's mad at me she calls me Patrick. Other times it's Pat," he explained, with a bright smile.

"Good. Whenever I call you Patrick here, at the Boys and Girls Club, let it serve as a warning that something is not quite right between us," I offered for his consideration.

"Sure thing, Bernard," the boy mocked, playfully.

"By the way, Pat. Never make a promise you can't keep," I concluded.

High five handclasps were exchanged. This incident proved to be the start of a friendship that has lasted over eighteen years.

Empty Promises

How many times have we heard the promise, "Wait until we get home," growled at a troublesome youngster, in a public place, by an agitated adult?

This is one of the most frequently used promises. Parents, grandparents, siblings, friends, coaches, managers, caregivers, and just about everyone else uses this promise to warn uncooperative youngsters.

The threat of some unknown retribution implied in this phrase has a calming effect on the mischief-maker, up to a point. In most cases it is regarded as an "empty promise/threat" that is generally meaningless. The child to whom this promise has been made repeatedly is aware from experience that it's empty.

By the time shopping is completed, the bill has been paid, the packages carried into the house, the intention of the threat "wait until we get home" has diminished in significance and thus often remains unfulfilled.

Social Promises

Care must be taken to ensure that our speech is not peppered with promises that can be dismissed as "empty bribes and/or hollow threats."

Their use to foster the achievement of a specific goal, be they of an academic, political, sport, or social nature, is ill-advised and unconscionable. One should take into account the limitations of the individual who is the target of such action.

Youngsters accept and remember promises. Some see them as a solemn pledge and work hard to attain and even surpass the adults' expectations.

The tragedy comes when community adults make social/political promises in the full knowledge that they will not or cannot be fulfilled. The effect on the citizenry is devastating and results in a profound lack of trust and increased level of cynicism.

People view such promises as being "conned." The tragic result is that in many cases individuals are not given the opportunity to realize their full potential. Consequently, both the individual and society are the big losers.

Elected leaders make social/political promises and create expectations in areas of housing, taxation, food, education, health services, family support, employment, child care and others. Many of these promises are made, in whole or in part, with the full knowledge that they are beyond society's means or ability to deliver.

The result is a dramatic increase in social dropouts. People, regardless of age, feel betrayed, inept, unimportant, undeserving, lost, and befuddled by the emptiness and sham of so many social promises.

By their reaction the disillusioned provide a continuing reminder of the failure of social promises. They run away and live on the streets, escaping through alcohol or drug-induced stupors, suicide, crime and other anti-social activity.

It is never too late to turn matters and bad habits around. This can be accomplished in great part by making the kind of personal and social promises we can individually and collectively honour.

A promise made and a promise kept is in fact a matter of being honest to oneself, each other, and the community.

Commentary:

- Broken promises tend to have a devastating effect on young children and youth.
- A history of broken promises often results in mistrust and despair.
- Promises that are kept tend to build trust, confidence, relationships, respect, communication, values and goals—the effects of which could last a lifetime.

ALL FOR ONE . . .

Empowering young people, regardless of age, to do the correct thing is a constant challenge. Once in a while a "teachable moment" occurs that provides an opportunity to underscore the need for individual responsibility and collective accountability. The following was one of those moments.

Upon my arrival in the "Dustbowl," where the skateboarding took place, I noticed that two older boys were not using safety equipment.

"Hold everything!" I demanded, following a blast on my whistle.

"Who's that guy?" an individual without safety equipment asked.

"That's Bernie . . ." "He's in charge . . ." "He teaches us stuff . . ." were examples of the spontaneous comments from other skateboarders.

My command, "Sit on it!" brought everything to a stop. All of the skateboarders obliged and sat on their boards with the exception of the two teenagers without safety gear.

"My name's Bernie, what's yours?"

"Marc," he smiled.

"And?" I asked, pointing at the second teen.

"Andrew. Er . . . it's our first time here."

"Very good. Glad to have you here. But when you are told 'sit on it,' don't continue to ride your board or lean against the wall."

Both slid their backs down the wall to sit on their skateboards.

"Thank you."

"You're welcome." responded Andrew.

"Shhh!" other boarders demanded.

"At the Club we have some safety rules. As you can see, Andrew, all the skateboarders are wearing helmets, elbow pads and knee pads."

"We didn't know."

"Andrew. One look at these guys, wearing safety equipment, should have rung a bell in your head. It's so obvious! You're both welcome to stay, but no riding your skateboards without the safety equipment. Okay?"

"We understand," Marc replied.

"As for the rest of you," I said, casting my hand in the direction of the others in attendance, "you guys have some responsibility to tell new fellows about the safety equipment requirements. The next time I find anyone skating without safety gear I'll close the Dustbowl. Have I made myself clear?"

"Yes, Bernie." "Gee, that's not fair!" "Okay," they replied.

"You're not going to learn very much just sitting on those boards. Let's go!" I said, clapping my hands. "Get on with it."

Over the next two and a half hours I instructed both ramp and rail slides by offering tips and manoeuvres to experienced skateboarders to enhance their performance. In addition the beginners sought instruction in the basic "free-style tricks" of this sport. Other Club members arrived, put on their safety gear without any reminder, and participated in this very popular activity.

This "hands-on" interaction in the Skateboard Program provided me with a positive alternative to my many administrative duties.

"Okay, guys. Enjoy yourselves," was my parting remark on leaving the Dustbowl.

Several hours later I looked in on the skateboarding activities. From my position in the doorway I observed Andrew and Marc riding the ramps, once again without any safety equipment.

"The Dustbowl will be closed immediately," I announced after a blast from my ever-present whistle.

"Bernie, how come? It's only two o'clock," young Brandon inquired after glancing at his watch.

"Because you, and most of these other fellows, were here earlier when I said that the Dustbowl would be closed if you let anyone skateboard without equipment. Correct?"

"Yes! But Bernie—"

"Remove your equipment now," I said, cutting off any further protest by Brandon.

From the groans and mumbled comments several dozen members were clearly unhappy with this sudden turn of events. Slowly they proceeded to remove their gear. In the meantime I blocked a quick exit of Andrew and Marc, by refusing to move out of the doorway.

"The least you two could do is to have the grace to apologize for what you've done."

"Sorry," Marc stated.

"What the heck did we do?" an incredulous Andrew demanded.

"Shut up, Andrew," demanded Marc.

"That's all right, Marc. I'll be happy to explain. First: You should be saying sorry to all those guys for being the cause of having the Dustbowl closed." I pointed to the fellows who were removing their safety equipment.

He looked at the other youngsters and with a smirk on his face, just shrugged his shoulders.

"Second: you were informed, by me, in no uncertain terms, that there was to be no skateboarding without wearing safety equipment."

"So?" Andrew sneered.

"Third: Should you have fallen and sustained a serious injury that could have been prevented, your parents would be asking why the Club allowed you to participate without safety equipment. Furthermore, steps could then be taken to close this very popular activity. Do you understand?"

"But we didn't injure ourselves . . . Did we?" Andrew snapped.

"You have totally missed the point."

"What point?" he demanded.

"Safety equipment, sir. Wear safety equipment."

"He got it. We both got your point." Marc advised.

"Excuse me, please?" Brandon asked.

"Hold on a moment, Brandon. We will all leave together and wait in the bottom of the stairwell. Is that understood by everyone?"

"Yes." "Okay." "What for?" some youngsters commented.

As the group assembled in the stairwell, Marc and Andrew ran up the flight of stairs leading to the front door of the clubhouse.

"Pay attention, please. Did I not say that the Dustbowl would be closed?" I asked shutting the door with a resounding thud.

The group let out a collective groan as some of them slowly headed for the stairs.

"Now that's been done. I guess it's time to reopen the Dustbowl for those skateboarders who will wear safety equipment. What do you guys say?" I teasingly jingled the large bundle of keys that are clipped to my belt.

"Wow, man!" "Sure thing, Bernie." "Yes, please!" they replied.

So it was that once the Dustbowl was reopened I took a few minutes to explain how each and every one of them has the responsibility to do what's in the best interest of the group.

"Raise your hand if any of you told those guys, Andrew and Marc, about our rule to wear safety gear."

No one raised a hand.

"Then by not speaking up you endorsed their actions."

"What's that mean?" Brandon asked.

"We are to blame. It's something like The Three Musketeers. All for one," Eddy, an experienced skateboarder, explained.

"And one for all," another boy added.

"They would kill us if we said anything." Brandon shot back.

"Eddy's right. This is your program. If you, your friends and visitors ride these ramps and rails without equipment and get hurt, you place those fellows and our club at risk. So speak up about the safety equipment requirements. Do you understand?"

"But what if they don't listen to us, Bernie?" Eddy asked.

"First: You don't know that they will not pay attention until you remind them to use safety equipment. Second: Speaking up shows them that you have their and your best interests in mind. Third: Should they persist and ride with no equipment, then you—each and every one of you—have a responsibility to bring that matter to the attention of the person in charge."

"But what if you're not here, Bernie?" Brandon interjected.

"Tell another staff," Eddy advised.

"Eddy's right. All of the staff agree that safety gear *must* be worn at all times when skateboarding. By asking guys to wear it, or by letting staff know when it's not being used, you are protecting what is now the only year-round skateboarding facility in the Ottawa–Carleton area."

"The only one?" a boy exclaimed.

"Yes. So fellows, your voice is just as important as mine—maybe even more important—when telling guys, be they large or small, to use safety equipment. Otherwise you are likely to lose all this." I underscored my words by making a sweeping arm motion around the room.

"Understand?"

"Yeah! We'll tell them," Brandon boasted, much to the amusement of the other skateboarders.

Commentary:

- With very few exceptions, there was no difficulty in having skateboarders comply with such an obvious common-sense requirement.

- Our skateboarders developed a "culture" for safety both in and away from our Club facilities.

- Empowerment of the individual or a group can be a tool for good or evil, depending on the motivation.

- Skateboarders brought honour and appreciation to themselves and our club, with the Canadian Championship and skill demonstrations for thousands of spectators during Canada Day celebrations and other community events.

CHILDREN LIVE WHAT THEY LEARN

The Negative:

Children living with criticism	Develop low self-esteem.
A youngster living with hostility	Learns aggression.
Adolescents living with ridicule	Become shy and withdrawn.
Children who live with shame	Develop feelings of guilt.
Those condemned to live in poverty	Learn anger and contempt.
When adults do not assert themselves	Children will take charge.
Constant predictions of failure	Are rewarded with failure.
Children living with war and conflict	Learn to take revenge.

The Positive:

Youngsters living with tolerance	Learn to be patient.
Children reared with loving care	Learn to be affectionate.
One who receives encouragement	Develops self-confidence.
Youth who receive praise	Learn to appreciate.
Adolescents who experience fairness	Understand justice.
Those who receive "Thank you"	Appreciate gratitude.
A secure child	Cultivates trust and peace.
Youngsters who enjoy friendships	Will find love in the world.
A child with goals and objectives	Has a route to success in life.

PART IV

Human Interest
& Humour

VICEREGAL PROTECTOR . . . ?

Visualize the bright lights of a television news crew; the excitement of the high school band; the restlessness of 300 club members; the expectation of local, provincial and national leaders of the Boys Club movement; the pride of civic leaders; the satisfaction of donors; and the sense of accomplishment by the volunteer board of directors of the Club, as the wife of the Governor General of Canada took centre stage for an historic ceremony.

Once Her Excellency Madam Leger, wife of the governor general of Canada, who served as patron of Boys Clubs of Canada, had assumed her place on the dais, the band played the "Viceregal Salute."

Mr. A. del Panet, president of the Ottawa club, explained that this ceremony was to celebrate the official change in the name, "Boys Clubs of Canada" to "Boys and Girls Clubs of Canada."

Following a brief statement of appreciation to the many donors who had underwritten the cost of constructing the Fred C. McCann Clubhouse, Her Excellency was invited to step forward and unveil the new name sign.

Christmas party in the grand ballroom of Rideau Hall. Governor General and Madame Jules Leger are surrounded by 150 excited young guests.

Courtesy of The Ottawa Citizen

Above her head was a "Boys Clubs of Canada" sign and official logo. As Her Excellency reached up to pull the silk tasselled cord the whole audience fell silent. As the new "Boys and Girls Club of Canada" banner unfolded, the calm atmosphere was disrupted with one resounding "Boo!" Immediately it was drowned out by prolonged applause, and music by the band.

From my vantage point at the edge of the stage I scanned the set of bleachers in which the Club members were seated. I observed the heads to my right were looking to their left and all the heads to my left were turned to their right. At their intersecting point sat Dwane, from the Centre Town Clubhouse. His gaze was downcast.

"It was Dwane!" "Dwane did it." "Dwane is going to get it from Bernie," were examples of the comments I heard as I made my way to confront this ill-mannered thirteen-year-old boy.

"I'll deal with you later, young man," I hissed through clenched teeth when I came to a stop in front of Dwane.

"Yes, sir. Sorry, Bernie," he said with a shrug of his shoulders, a look of bewilderment on his red flushed face.

"It is way too late for apologies, Dwane. You had better behave yourself for the rest of this evening," I demanded.

Dwane nodded his head in consent.

It was my duty to accompany Her Excellency throughout the next hour and introduce her to donors, alumni, community leaders, Youth Council members, Junior Leaders Corps and the "Boys and Girls of the Year" from each of our clubhouses. Either by accident or design, Dwane seemed to be on the fringes of each group we approached.

I started to introduce club members at random to Her Excellency, being careful to avoid Dwane no matter where he popped up in the crowd.

"Why is it not the Girls and Boys Club of Canada? Girls first, you know!" a teenage girl asked Madam Leger.

"I will leave that question for Mr. Muzeen to answer," the viceregal lady said, turning to me with a smile.

"Well it's in alphabetical order. 'B' comes before 'G.' Also on any list of community agencies our name, as it presently stands, would be situated near the top of such a listing," was my reply.

"Oh. I see," the teenager exclaimed.

Dwane's "Hi, Bernie!" greeting was ignored by me as I turned, with my special guest, and walked towards the official party gathered on the stage.

"Who was that young man?"

"Dwane, Your Excellency. He is the boy who booed after you pulled the cord to change the name sign. I will be dealing with him later!" I assured her.

"I must have a word with him. Please . . ." she stated, while doing an about turn, coming face-to-face with Dwane.

While Her Excellency talked to him in a hushed voice that I could not hear, from where I was standing, the boy smiled occasionally while maintaining eye contact with me, by looking over Her Excellency's shoulder. Following a gentle pat on Dwane's arm by Her Excellency, the boy gave her his undivided attention, nodding in apparent agreement with what she was saying.

Moments later, both of them shook hands, and broke into gales of laughter at another witty remark made by Her Excellency, I presume.

"What will happen to Dwane?" Her Excellency inquired.

"Not to worry, Madam. That will be determined when he returns to our Centre Town Clubhouse," I replied.

"That's what worries Dwane. I assured him that I did not hear his boos. Please promise me you will forget it happened?" she asked gently.

"But Madam . . . !" I exclaimed.

"Now, Mr. Muzeen. I want you to consider that Dwane is under my protection from now on." She raised her voice just enough so that the bane of the moment could hear the viceregal command.

The ceremony over, our guest of honour returned to Rideau Hall.

In the weeks, months, and years to follow Dwane would invoke "viceregal protection" to rescue himself from my perceived wrath, whenever he or his friends felt they were in a conflict situation. It forced both of us to develop a relationship of mutual trust and confidence that was to last for many happy years.

Commentary:

- It proved to be a great object lesson "that everyone has someone else to answer to," regardless of how much power they may perceive that they have over the conduct, behaviour, or lives of others.
- Those being led need to understand that even their leader is answerable to a "higher power."
- "Pardons," be they formal or informal, can be powerful tools to encourage behaviour modification in citizens of all ages.

A LITTLE MUD WON'T HURT

"I thought you people would look after my little boy," a woman said to the front desk attendant.

"Did you check him in to the Club today?" he asked, flipping through the daily attendance record.

"No. I just dropped him off at the park, across the street."

"We will look around the clubhouse to see if he's here. What's his n—?"

"Trevor." She cut the attendant off in mid-sentence. "And he's standing outside your front door in the rain!" an agitated tone in her voice.

Hearing this exchange through the open door of my office, I decided to see if there was anything I could do.

"Hello. I'm Bernie. Can I be of assistance?"

"Yes. I'm Debby Dunlap. My boy Trevor . . ." her voice trailed away as she motioned towards the front door. "He's a real mess. I don't know what I am going to do. I got off work at 2:30 p.m. so we could go shopping. Now . . . !" was her frustrated comment, bringing her right hand to her face.

"Where is Trevor?" I enquired with a smile.

"He's covered in mud . . . out there," she replied sternly, pointing to several youngsters standing in the rain.

Walking to the front door I observed several boys, nine to eleven years of age, covered from head to foot with mud.

"My goodness!" was my immediate reaction. "Which one of you is Trevor?"

A slightly built lad raised his hand as mud oozed down his arm.

"Hi, Trevor. Come here." I beckoned with my index finger.

The boy remained where he stood, alternating looking from his mother and to me several times.

"Come here." I pointed to the space between his mother and me.

A smile of pearly white teeth lit up a mud-splattered face.

Mockingly wiping his feet on the concrete steps leading to the clubhouse, Trevor obeyed my instructions.

"The next time you have a mud fight include me, okay, Trevor?"

"Yeah!" he exclaimed.

"Was it fun?"

Mrs. Dunlap scowled at me as her son nodded his head vigorously.

"Why don't you go shopping, Mrs. Dunlap. We will clean Trevor and his friends up in the meantime. He can stay here until five p.m. That gives us time to find clothes for him and the other boys," I proposed.

"Well he's not a member, and . . ." His mother glanced at her watch.

"Don't worry, Mrs. Dunlap. Trevor is allowed up to three visits before taking out a Club membership," I assured her.

"Well! If he would like to . . ." She took a long look at her son.

"Sure, Mum! That's great!" he said, answering her unfinished question.

"I will not be too long, dear. You be good," said a relaxed mother as she made her way to the family car. "Thank you. I will be back by five," she added, looking back in my direction.

Her son and mud-covered playmates waved farewell as the car turned onto Percy Street.

"Trevor, how old are you?"

"Nine," he responded shyly.

"Are you here with friends?"

"No. We met here," he said, gesturing at the boys who were still standing on the sidewalk in front of the clubhouse.

"How is the mud, fellows?" I inquired, approaching the group.

"Okay, I guess . . ." "Fine . . ." "Sticky . . ." they mumbled.

"What the heck do you think you are, a bunch of hippopotamuses?"

The serious expressions that masked their faces, along with the mud, vanished in broad smiles.

"Trevor, get out here so Len can hose you down. By the way, have you heard the song, 'Mud, Mud . . . Glorious mud . . . Nothing like it for cooling the blood?' Don't you know it?" I said, knocking a clump of mud from the head of a boy I now recognized to be Donald. "What do you think, Donald?"

From the pained expression on his face I was not sure if it was my singing, or the words of a strange song, that caused his reaction.

Wiping mud from his face Donald whispered, " My mum will kill me if I go home like this."

"Let Len hose you down. While you're in the shower I will round up some replacement clothing for you fellows."

"Gee thanks, Bernie," was their collective response.

As Len connected the hose and the boys started scraping mud off each other, I made my way to a collection of donated children's clothing to select items for these youngsters.

"When you are all clean, dressed and tidy, come to my office."

About forty minutes later, Trevor, Donald, Marc, Carl and Jason entered my office. A larger group of members had gathered in the hallway.

"Thanks for the clothes, Bernie," Donald said, as he motioned his companions to be seated around my worktable.

"When are we going to have the mud fight?" Carl asked.

"Because when we have it we are going to get you, Bernie, right guys?" Donald boasted.

A cheer came from the youngsters in the front hall.

"What on earth are you talking about?" I demanded a puzzled look on my face.

"Come off it, Bernie," demanded thirteen-year-old Jim standing in the doorway. "We're going to get you good during the mud fight," he stated as he looked around at his cheering friends.

"Get serious. Where did you get such a crazy idea?" I laughed.

"That new guy . . ." Donald pointed to Trevor. "You told him."

"Donald . . . Fellows! I was only joking. Isn't that correct, Trevor?" turning to the new boy for support.

"No!" Trevor shouted. Looking around he took a deep breath, adding, "You said we could have a mud fight. You said you would be there. You said that to me and my mother . . . !" he insisted, pointing his finger at me accusingly.

"I know what I said. Don't point at me!" I snapped.

Watching the crestfallen expression on his face and responding to a collective groan from the other boys, I added, "It was only a joke."

"But it would be fun, Bernie," intoned Marc, rubbing the palms of his hands together in happy anticipation.

"What would?" I asked with a smile, fully knowing the answer.

"A mud fight with *you*," he beamed.

"Yeah! A little mud won't hurt you!" exclaimed Donald.

"Donald!" I said with a scowl.

"We want a mud fight," he repeated several times. Other members picked up his chant. They marched up and down the length of the front hall and around the table in my office, all good-naturedly, for several minutes. Their demonstration attracted additional youngsters who were otherwise preparing to go home.

"Come on, Bernie. Let the little fellows have their mud fight. Phil and I will be on your side," sixteen-year-old Luke proposed, joining the group in my office.

Looking at the happy, expectant and excited faces of the children, I swallowed hard and heard myself saying, "Okay, guys. You can have a mud fight, but . . ."

A resounding cheer drowned out the last part of my statement. Luke and Phil, two popular senior Club members, were mobbed by Donald, Marc and the other youngsters.

Luke brought the group to order by shouting, "Guys, hold it! Bernie had not finished his answer before you all cut him off."

He gave me a thumbs-up and a broad smile.

"Thank you, Luke. As I was about to say before I was interrupted: Okay, guys, we will have your mud fight—next summer."

"Err . . ." "Not fair . . ." "You're Chicken . . . !" were some of the assorted comments from the clearly disappointed children.

"Come on, fellows! We have only one week left in this summer's program and all our special events have been scheduled. If we are going to have a mud fight it will have to be next year. Take it or forget about it," I commanded.

The group let out an unexpected lusty cheer.

"Next year you're going to get it, Bernie. Right, guys?" Another joyful cheering drowned out the remainder of Donald's comment.

The ringing of the bell announcing that the clubhouse was closing for the day thankfully brought a swift conclusion to their demonstration.

"Next year, guys, I'm going to get each and every one of you" was my reply to their challenge.

"Oh, yeah!" several boys said brazenly.

"Yeah!" was my attempt to have the last word on this subject as the Club members headed home.

As promised, the *Calendar of Special Events for Summer 1973* featured a members vs. staff **mud fight.**

On the appointed day the baseball field across the street from the clubhouse was soaked down with water to create a substantial mud patch. The mud fight, which attracted extensive coverage by the local media, was scheduled to start at 1:30 p.m. Much to my dismay I was the only staff person willing to participate.

My co-workers had found a number of excuses not to be involved.

Nevertheless, two dozen Club members and I had a most enjoyable time. We were all amazed at the extent of the newspaper and TV news coverage this event garnered.

Annual mud fight, which proved to be a highlight of the summer program, provided mud-happy youngsters an opportunity to let Bernie have it!

Courtesy of The Ottawa Citizen

In the years that followed, our fun-filled mud fight, which at times involved over fifty youngsters and half a dozen staff, brought local and national recognition to our Boys and Girls Club movement due to media coverage.

An unexpected benefit was our club's immediate recognition when it came to membership recruitment and fundraising projects.

There were other benefits:

The Club was shown to be a fun place to prospective members.

A "good news story" demonstrated to children and youth that *they* would be the centre of attention while having fun.

Participants were provided an opportunity to release pent-up energy.

Members and staff were shown interacting.

Given that Club members planned their vacation at Camp Minwassin so as not to miss the annual mud fight at the Club, a mud pit was created at the camp.

The community, through the media, was made aware of the new and current programs the Club offered.

Several alumni expressed concern that the mud fight was not the kind of event that the CEO of the Club should engage in. It would "demean the position" in the view of the general public. Feedback proved this position to be an unfounded overreaction.

On balance with other special events such as: Police Fun Night, the World Bubble Gum Blowing Championship, the Viceregal Christmas Party, multi-cultural festivals, snow wars, skateboarding demonstrations, Awards and Recognition Night, and Service Club Fun Days, the Mud Fight was a good fit with the year-round activities for our Boys and Girls Club.

THEM'S THE BREAKS

While doing my spring cleaning, I stepped back to admire the tremendous cleaning job I had done on the sunroom windows, forgetting that I was nine inches above the ground! The realization of my forgetfulness was driven home with the crack of my anklebone. This required a visit to the hospital for X-rays and the installation of a toe-to-knee plaster cast.

When I showed up at the clubhouse in a wheelchair, youngsters competed with each other to push my chair, fetch me cold drinks, and to have the opportunity to sign my leg cast.

A number of youngsters were incredulous that I, of all people, would break a leg. A few found my predicament to be mildly amusing. Still others expressed the view that only a broken leg would slow me down for a while. In very short order, my leg cast was covered with a mass of names, good wishes and artwork of Club members.

While they signed my cast, I responded to enquiries as to how I broke my leg. In some cases, a child may have stood in line and heard everything I had shared with the preceding member. Nevertheless, each child would insist on being told the whole story. On several occasions, young listeners corrected me because what I had told them did not match what I may have told a previous child.

I learned from this brief episode that children are acute listeners and pick up minor deviations from what is supposed to be "the truth."

I also took great delight in cautioning the youngsters about the dangers of doing housework. They were advised that housekeeping was the kind of activity that should be left exclusively to their parents. The reason being that parents should not place children at risk by having them do those kinds of tasks.

"Housework is something that children should abstain from undertaking," I would preach. Needless to say, the Club members found that they could fully agree with my point of view.

It was great fun. I delighted in the response of my young friends. It did much to deflect my attention from the discomfort of my broken leg.

With tongue sunk deeply in my cheek, I advised eleven-year-old Chris to refuse to do any housework. "It is your right to be properly trained before you practise housework. Without such training, Chris, how can you be prevented from sustaining a serious injury such as mine?" Chris and his friends laughed uproariously during our Thursday afternoon exchange.

You can imagine my mixture of shock and amusement when I received a telephone call from Chris's mother the following Monday morning. "What are you telling those kids at the Boys and Girls Club? What kind of ideas are you putting into their heads, Bernie?" she demanded.

"I don't understand, what you mean, Mrs. Lalonde," I countered.

"We have been fighting with Chris all weekend to clean up his room. He says that you told him that it is dangerous work, and that he could hurt himself," she explained. "I can't take any more of this, Bernie."

"Why, that little devil. It is true I broke my leg doing housework last week. I was jokingly telling the Club members, including Chris, that they should not do any housework for fear they would injure themselves. But it was told to them in fun. As a joke!" I just could not help but smile to myself as I talked with Chris's mother.

"Well, it's no joke around this home," Mrs. Lalonde cut in.

"May I speak to Chris, please?" I asked with some apprehension.

"Hi, Bernie?" said a perky voice.

"What the heck are you doing, young man?" I demanded of this usually meek, soft-spoken boy.

"Oh. Having some fun with Mum," he said, with a chuckle.

"She does not seem to see the humour of this situation, buddy."

"I know. That's what makes it so funny," he laughed. "Them's the breaks, Bernie," he teased.

"Chris. Are you coming to the Club today?" I asked, trying my best not to burst out laughing. This boy had just shown me another side of his personality.

"Yeah," was his matter-of-fact reply.

"Then do us a both a favour. Clean up your room before leaving home, please."

"Sure thing. But you should have seen Mum, Bernie. It was so funny," he explained, with a chuckle.

"Chris. I am sure it was. But will you please clean up your room before you come to the Club?"

"Oh sure, Bernie, no problem." The boy was clearly enjoying himself.

"Okay, Chris. Put your dear mother back on the line, please?" I requested.

Mrs. Lalonde's tone of voice was much more pleasant when she said with a laugh, "Bernie, I know that I have told Chris and his sister to listen to you and to what you say. But I tell you I never expected this. I can see how it might have been funny to Chris, but throughout the weekend it did not seem very funny to me!"

"Mrs. Lalonde, Chris has assured me that the joke has ended," I explained. "I am sorry about this. I just did not expect Chris or any other club member to take my humorous advice seriously. I sure hope I don't have other mothers telephoning me today!"

"Thanks, Bernie," she laughed.

When Chris arrived at the clubhouse, he had a grin from ear to ear. He made a point of stopping by my office.

"Well. Did you clean up your room?"

"Sure I did, Bernie. You can phone my mother," he challenged, as he pointed to the telephone on my desk.

At that point our eyes met. We both started to laugh and laugh heartily at my predicament.

I now realized that the joke was on me. "Gosh, those kids don't show me any respect," was my bemused conclusion.

SENSITIVE SITUATIONS

The problem of racial and cultural prejudice has permeated just about every level of community life.

Circumstances have placed me in situations where I have seen the results of insensitive and mindless remarks made without a second thought as to their injurious effect. Mindless slurs often degenerate into bigotry, prejudice and discrimination.

These remarks hurt the listener, poison relationships, create fear, and contribute to the construction of an invisible wall of words that divides people and their community.

This negative mindset has to be constantly challenged. Such action requires individuals to confront discrimination, whether it's a matter of colour, culture, religion or gender.

To ignore the bigots, or to laugh along with their cruel jokes, could be perceived as tacit approval of their negative mindset.

In over forty years of social and community service I have learned that the personal integrity of individual citizens is the best antidote to bigotry and prejudice.

The following are examples of bigoted or sensitive situations that I have attempted to resolve with truth, reality, common sense and humour.

A Question of Colour

After repeatedly trying to bring some sixty youngsters to order while suffering from a bad case of laryngitis, I invited Ronnie, a thirteen-year-old Club member, to assist.

"Ronnie, would you please tell that boy in the green sweater that I am waiting for him to pay attention?" I gasped.

Looking about the unfinished room, in the basement of the Centre Town Clubhouse, known as the "Dustbowl," Ronnie asked, "Bernie, do you mean that black kid?"

"I mean the boy in the green sweater," was my whispered reply.

"Hi, Marcus. Pay attention to Bernie," Ronnie called.

Following the announcement I took Ronnie aside and asked "Why did you refer to Marcus by the colour of his skin, rather than by the colour of his sweater?"

"Doesn't everyone?" was the boy's casual response.

"Well, next time please refer to Club members by their name, the game they are playing or by the colour of their clothes. Not by the colour of their skin," I entreated.

"Oh sure," the boy said, with a shrug of the shoulders as he returned to playing with his friends.

Commentary:

- We need children to recognize each other for what they are . . . *children*.

- Racial and or slang terms to describe one another are totally unacceptable.

- Given that adults have poisoned the thought processes of our children, the task before us is not an easy one.

I Had to Tell the Truth

Walking down the stairs of the Parliament Building following the "Cherish the Children Concert," which had been held in the reading room of the central block to commemorate National Child's Day, a young man fell in step with me.

"Hi, Bernie," he said.

"Hallo. Did you enjoy the show?"

"Sure. By the way, Bernie, do you remember that little incident I had with your blue station wagon?" my young escort inquired.

"Hum. Which incident?" I asked, as my mind raced through a whole series of events that my car has suffered, over the years. They included: water bombing; a tire blow-out; sour milk bath; the jacking up of the car and removal of its four wheels; and removal of the air valves from the tires, among others.

"Remember? I'm Richard. About six years ago I drove your station wagon into a tree, at Camp Minwassin?"

"You. My God. I have wanted to talk to you about that. Who was that other fellow?"

"Patrick. Pat was helping you and me close up Camp Minwassin, for the winter. He was about nineteen years old, I think."

"Yes. That's right. In fact I ran into Pat a couple of months ago. He's doing well, with a full-time job . . ." I faded to silence.

We walked towards my car. "How are you getting home, Rich?"

"By bus, I guess."

"No way. Let me drive you. I have to go west. I can drop you off at Coldwell Avenue. I take it that you still live there? I may even have a quick visit with your mother. Is she still there?"

"Yes. Mum's still there. But me, I live two blocks away."

I playfully offered Richard the keys to my car.

"I don't think so," my young companion countered, a look of mock horror on his face.

We got into the car. "Richard, it is great seeing you. I would like to get together with you and learn how the accident happened; whether Pat was involved; how you felt about it; how long it took you to come and tell me. There are other questions as to how that incident affected our relationship. What do you think about that, buddy?"

"When? When would you like to do this?"

"In the next day or two. Maybe over dinner?"

"Okay with me, Bernie," Richard replied, eagerly.

"I remember every detail as if it had just happened," he added, as I drove off the Hill.

Several days later we had an enjoyable turkey dinner. On that occasion Richard and I shared the following insights.

"Bernie, did you know when you gave me your car keys, that it was my first time behind the steering wheel by myself?"

"Not really. But then why do you think I warned you to drive carefully? By the way, Richard, you're not the first feller I've let drive my car. Other than Pat and I, you were the only other person in camp. What could go wrong?"

My young guest chuckled at this rhetorical question.

"I think it started, Bernie, because you wanted Patrick to know what time supper would be served. Anyway, after at least an hour of practice driving in the ball field the day before with you I was feeling real confident. I then drove past the Swamp Cabin, when I saw Patrick."

"He waved. I stopped and he got into the car. We were heading for your cottage, for supper, but I wanted to drive a bit more. So I drove past the trail that leads to the camp director's cottage and up the camp road to the main gate."

"Then what?"

"I didn't want to turn that big car around, on the road, as there were ditches on each side. Plus I wanted practice driving in reverse. Pat just stared forward. I guessed he was confident in me as well. So I put my arm around the passenger seat, looked back and hit the gas. I don't know how it happened, but your car rolled up on one side of the road, and when I tried to fix the situation I overcorrected and went to the other side of the road. Picture lots of trees on either side of the road. Yes. You've got it," Rich paused, and gave me a fleeting smile.

"What was Pat doing?"

"Patrick wasn't looking ahead any more. We both slowly got out of your car to see the prize—a dent—in the rear bumper. The bumper was wrapped around the tree trunk."

Taking two long gulps of milk from his glass, Richard continued. "It took quite a bit of gas to get the car off the tree and start the trek back to your cottage."

"Richard, you mean to say that you came right back to the cottage?"

"Well, not really. Had Patrick not been in the car with me I'd have probably taken a long time to return to the cottage."

"How long did it take you to get up the courage to return and tell me?"

"About twenty minutes, I think."

"Really?"

"To relieve my guilt feelings I felt sure you wouldn't get mad. That you understood that accidents happen. Besides, I was also only fifteen at the time. So how could I get into trouble, as I wasn't even supposed to be driving?"

"Did Pat tell you what to say?"

"Not really. Patrick drove back to the cottage because I was so scared. He advised me to tell you straightforwardly what had happened. As we approached the cottage I could feel my stomach in my mouth. The guilt I felt, after you had trusted me with the second most valuable thing a person usually owns. I just knew that I had to tell the truth."

"Oh really. How come?"

"Bernie. You must remember that I had known you for about ten years. After all, you had let me join the Boys and Girls Club when I was only five years old."

"So?"

"I had been in trouble before with you over the years. Of course nothing this serious. Anyway, I learned that the best way to deal with you, when I was in trouble, was to tell the truth. Don't care what kind of trouble, always tell you the truth, first time."

"How come?"

"You were much easier to deal with. Besides, Bernie, you also had a knack of finding out the truth. It was amazing."

"What did you think my action would be, Richard?"

"I figured it would be all mixed up. Like you would yell at me; I would never be trusted; you would hold a grudge against me; that I would have to go home right away; I'd not benefit from our friendship that I had enjoyed since I was five; you would tell my mother; you would get real angry. That kind of stuff."

"That's very interesting to know."

I poured a cup of tea before responding to my guest. "When you walked through the door of the cottage I knew something serious had happened."

"Really. How come?"

"First of all you held the car keys straight out in front of you. Your face was ashen, the colour of your lips had faded and your extended arm trembled. Clearly something serious had happened. I just knew that I had to remain calm."

"Wow!"

"Richard. Do you recall my reaction?"

"First you asked if Patrick and I were hurt. Then you asked us to go outside and inspect the damage. After we did that you told me not to worry and returned to the cottage to serve the supper that you had cooked. When I said I was sorry you told me that you did not wish to have it mentioned again."

"Did that surprise you?"

"Not really. I did share with Patrick how quickly you blew the incident away. You said not to mention it. That's what you wanted, that's what you got. Then we spent the rest of the weekend working at Camp."

"When I dropped you off at home, were you expecting me to go in and tell your mother about what you did to my car?"

"No. I just knew you would not go back on your word. So I told her all about it."

"When?"

"That Sunday night."

"Well done, Richard. I'm proud of you, buddy."

"Bernie, did the insurance pay for those repairs?"

"Certainly not. I replaced the bumper at my own expense."

"Oh my God. Now I do feel guilty," Richard said, with a touch of incredulity to his voice.

"Please don't worry about it, my friend."

"This is great. Here we are, six years later and still good friends."

"And there is no reason why our friendship should not continue for many years to come, Richard," I assured him.

"Sure thing, Bernie."

Commentary:

- Truth is like a shield or mantle. It is designed to protect and comfort those who use it.

- By overreacting to learning the truth, leaders can set in place a pattern of deceit, lies and misrepresentation that is hard to break; this can subsequently lead to difficulties for both parties.

- Leaders have to learn how to encourage telling the truth without compromising their ability to discipline offenders.

- Truth telling can be a stressful experience for both parties.

- Leaders need to be truthful with their charges, their organization and themselves.

- Children and youth are highly sensitive to the truthfulness of their leaders. It is a basis for building a positive relationship that could last a lifetime.

But He Doesn't Look Sixty-Five!

This short story involves Jason and Jeff, twelve-year-old boys who had been members of the Centre Town Clubhouse of the Boys and Girls Club of Ottawa–Carleton since they were six years of age. Needless to say, they got to know me very well over the years.

My attitude has been one of encouraging Club members, regardless of age, to develop a level of approachability coupled with informality that would allow them to initiate a conversation with me. Consequently, the children got to set the agenda of discussion and decide the topic they wished to discuss.

The results were, to say the least, amusing at times.

Shortly after my retirement as executive director/general manager of the Boys and Girls Club of Ottawa–Carleton had been announced in the media, Jeff and Jason engaged me in the following exchange, in the crowded lobby of the Centre Town Clubhouse.

"Bernie, is it true that you are you going to retire?" Jeff asked.

"How do you know that?" I enquired.

"It's in the newspaper."

"Oh. I see. Yes, it is true. I will be leaving at the end of the summer program, in August."

"Why?" Jason cut in.

"Why what?"

"Why are you retiring, Bernie?" he pressed.

"Well I have been here twenty-two years. Do you know that when I came here I gave the board of directors an undertaking to stay five years? It has now grown to over twenty years. The time has come to retire," I explained softly.

"But Bernie . . . you don't look *old* enough to retire!" Jeff almost shouted, with a touch of incomprehension to his voice.

For that kind remark I tousled his hair. "Thanks, buddy. You can say that again," and I struggled to keep control of my emotions.

There was a moment of uneasy quiet, as though the children were searching for the correct thing to say next.

"What's that to do with you guys?" I asked.

"Well," said Jeff, his eyes gleaming, "I hoped that you would stay for at least another six years. At least until I am eighteen years old."

I was deeply moved by this expression of trust and confidence. My eyes welled up. I turned towards my office door, in an attempt to get hold of myself.

As I opened the office door I heard these final remarks.

"Gee, Bernie's retiring . . ." a third voice said.

"Yes. At the end of the summer program!" Jeff explained.

"But he doesn't look sixty-five. He doesn't even look sixty," the third voice exclaimed.

The closing of the office door behind me cut off the remainder of that exchange. I found myself smiling inwardly, hoping the children meant that I looked younger than what they thought.

Commentary:

I have included this story because many adult friends thought it was humorous.

PART V

Conflict & Resolution

BLOOD BROTHERS

"There are two guys being rude to Winston in the games room," a twelve-year-old Club member stated, as he stood at the end of the worktable in my office.

"It's really bad, Bernie," his companion added from his position in the doorway.

"I really appreciate you guys letting me know about this. By the way, what happened to cause this outbreak of rude or smart remarks?" I asked, as if it were an afterthought.

Both boys scrunched their shoulders to indicate lack of knowledge.

I went to the games room where Winston worked as a part-time supervisor. All seemed to be in order.

Winston, at seventeen years of age, was a very popular individual due to his athletic ability and openhearted attitude towards Club members.

"Winston, I hear someone is being rude. If it continues I wish to know about it," I said quietly as I stood beside my co-worker.

"It's okay for now. Nothing I can't handle," he assured me.

With that assurance I went about supervising the Archery Club in the lower gym. An hour or so later I returned to my office and was about to leave for home when a couple of boys aged nine and eleven, followed by Winston, entered the office.

"These guys . . . they just will not listen . . . I have had just about all I can take," Winston said in exasperation.

In a quick glance at the two boys, I detected a smile on the face of the taller of the two boys.

"What's so funny, young man?" I thundered.

"It's him. He called Winston a 'spear chucker,'" said David, pointing at his chum, Chris.

"Oh yeah! You called him a 'jungle bunny,' David," he counter-charged with a big grin. The next moment both boys broke into a fit of repressed laughter.

I brought the palm of my hand down on the table with a loud bang.

"This is not funny. How dare you! How dare either of you be so rude to Winston or anyone else?" I demanded of the two startled boys. "Tell me, what gives you the right to be so cruel and crude?" I added forcefully.

With heads hanging and downcast eyes, the boys were shocked into silence.

"Look at me when I talk to you," I snapped.

Neither head moved.

"It is obvious that you cannot look at me because neither of you can explain your disgusting behaviour. Consequently, I will leave you in this office and expect you to explain yourselves to Winston. Is that clear?" I stated, as I shoved my chair away from the table around which they stood.

Two startled faces now looked up. The expression of disbelief was marked. David had tears in his eyes. Chris fixed me with narrow eyes and a tight-lipped expression.

"You three have exactly ten minutes to sort this out by yourselves. Winston, I would like you to share with Chris and David how it feels to be insulted by rude little boys because of the colour of your skin. As for you two, you had better be able to explain your unacceptable behaviour to Winston—if you can—then to me when I return," I said with a show of controlled annoyance as I headed for the door.

I pulled the office door shut with a dramatic thud in the hope that it would reinforce my message.

Upon walking into the gymnasium, Duncan challenged me to a badminton match. Ten minutes elapsed, then fifteen, and after twenty minutes and five games, of which Duncan won four, I headed back to my office.

Opening the door softly I found Winston seated with his arms like the protecting wings of a guardian angel around each of the boys.

The boys had their tearstained faces pressed against Winston's broad chest. They followed my every move as I made my way slowly to the large swivel chair at my desk.

I sat down in the oversized chair and remained silent.

The tension was broken by a deep sniffling from David.

"What do you think, Winston?" I asked softly.

"Oh . . . it's okay now," this self-assured high school student stated as he took a fond look at each of his young charges and gave them a squeeze.

"Bernie, David and Chris now know that they can really hurt someone by insulting them just because their skin colour is different. I have explained to these guys that they not only hurt me but my younger brother and my little sister with these kinds of crude remarks." Taking a deep breath he added, "Chris and Dave really understand. Don't you, guys?" all the while gently holding the boys protectively.

"What about you two! How about sitting down on chairs at the table and explaining to me what you have learned. I would also like to know how come you guys learned and used such rude and unacceptable names against another person," I said, pointing to the empty chairs on each side of Winston.

"Everyone says it," David explained as he took his place at the table.

"Who did you hear say something like that: Harry, Jim, Nancy, or maybe a teacher or even me? Come on, tell me who says it?" I pressed David, as I rolled my chair close to his side.

"Well not them. But I hear it all over," David spluttered as the tears started to flow.

"Calm down, David," I said softly, and ran my hand through his hair.

"How about you, Chris, do you hear any of the clubhouse staff use any of those terms?" I asked.

"No," was his whispered response.

"Then if the Club staff do not use those insults on you or other Club members, it is only fair to expect Club members not to use such insults on our staff?" I asked.

"I guess so," David sighed.

"By the way, Chris. Do your parents use these kinds of remarks at home?"

"No," the young boy snapped.

"Maybe a teacher at Centennial School?"

"No . . . not them," was his response.

"Chris . . . Let's say you were disabled, or another colour, or you spoke with an accent, such as I do. Would that give other guys the right to insult you and to make you unhappy?"

He shook his head.

"What was that you said, my young friend?"

"No," he hissed, as he shifted uncomfortably in his chair.

While the boy indicated a degree of discomfort with the subject being discussed, I was concerned that the message was not getting across to him.

I was determined to find another way to reach him.

"Hey, guys. Let's look at each of us. Don't we each have two eyes and two ears?" Their heads nodded in agreement.

"We also have hands, teeth, legs, feet, blood, and faces. The only problem is that none of you three guys are as good looking as me," I proposed, with a smile.

All present smiled. The tension was now broken. Perhaps the boys would be a little more receptive to the point being made.

"Fellows, you see that Winston has a different pigment to his skin. In fact I am jealous of Winston because he plays basketball better than me. But then, he cannot beat me at table tennis," I pushed ahead.

"Not for much longer, Bernie. Right, guys?" Winston retorted, as he sought the endorsement of the two boys.

"Chris, how is your younger brother? Oh . . . what's his name . . . that was in hospital, recently?"

"Eric. His name is Eric and he's okay," the boy said, with a puzzled expression on his upturned face.

"Just suppose Eric was ill. Very ill. That the only thing that could make him better was a blood transfusion. That the only person available with the correct type of blood was Winston. Would you give your little brother Winston's blood?" I inquired.

"Well, sure—I would want him to get better," Chris said, as he cast a shy smile in Winston's direction.

"Then surely, my young friend, we do not need to go around insulting the very people who could possibly help save the lives of those we love?"

"Yes," Chris responded, with a sense of realization.

"By the way, guys," I said, as I got out of my chair and reached for my overcoat. "If we all got a blood transfusion from Winston, would that make us all 'blood brothers'? You know, guys . . . I sure would not mind having any of you fellows as my brother."

There were handshakes and embraces all around. David and Chris headed off to play in the clubhouse. Winston assumed his duties in the games room. I headed home.

Commentary:

- There is a pressing need to provide children with an opportunity to appreciate and celebrate our differences.
- To this end a series of cultural festivals was developed by the Boys and Girls Club of Ottawa–Carleton in an attempt to help share the riches of the cultural backgrounds Canadians bring to the community.
- These cultural festivals were very helpful in heightening the awareness, understanding, appreciation and acceptance of the diversity and cultural backgrounds of other Club members.

THEY'RE RIPPED OFF

It was mid-December when a young man (we will call him John) came into my office and placed a package on my worktable. Since I was on the telephone, I gestured for him to wait until I had completed my call.

John sat in the chair at the head of the worktable. His eyes were fixed on the package.

"A Christmas present for me! Oh you shouldn't have, John," I said playfully as I rolled in my oversized chair from the desk to the table.

"What is it?" I asked, as I reached for the package.

"Pants," the boy replied without looking up.

"A gift for or from someone?"

"No. Not really," he intoned.

"A gift for yourself, then . . . ?"

"No, Bernie. They're ripped off," John said, as he made fleeting eye contact with me.

Without a word I reached over and took the package. Opening it up I found it contained two pairs of pants.

I took my time examining these pants. Then I looked over at the fourteen-year-old sitting in front of me and said "John, They're okay. I can't see any rip in either of the trousers."

He did not respond.

"Stand up, young man. Hold these against yourself," I demanded.

John did as he was requested without comment.

The pants were clearly several sizes too big.

I folded them neatly and placed them back in the shopping bag and slid them across the table, so that they came to rest in front of the teenager. His lower lip quivered in respond to my action.

"So what's upsetting you, my friend?"

"Well . . . I took 'em," John whispered.

"I beg your pardon?" I asked, cupping my ear with my right hand.

"I took 'em," he said, clearing his throat in an attempt to keep his emotions in check.

"So you took them and you brought them here. Why?"

He shrugged his shoulders.

"They are way too big for you, John. Just take them back."

"Look, Bernie . . . you don't understand—" John exclaimed.

I cut him off with, "John, I do understand. You told me these pants were ripped. I have examined them and they are not ripped. They're okay, so you take them back to the store and exchange them for the correct size."

There was a very long pause. His chin was on his chest.

When he raised his head to make eye contact with me, his face was white and he was biting his lower lip. With tear-filled eyes John whispered softly, "I stole them during the weekend."

It was clear that this teenager was trying to come to grips with the predicament that confronted him.

"Is that all you are going to tell me? Or are you going to tell me the name of the store from where you stole them and what you intend to do about it?"

"I stole them from X.Y.Z., Bank Street near Gladstone, on Saturday." John's eyes searched my face as if trying to anticipate my reaction.

"Then sir, you had better take them back," was my rejoinder.

With that the dam burst. Tears streamed down his face while his whole body shook in the chair at the other end of the table.

Getting out of my chair, I closed the office door and then sat in the chair next to John. I placed a firm hand on his shoulder in an attempt to reassure him that he was not alone.

I had known him as a trouble-free Club member for about seven years. All in all, he was basically a good boy.

"Okay, okay, John, let's calm down and figure out what we can do to resolve this situation."

It took a few moments and several deep breaths before John lifted his tearstained face and asked, "What can we do now?" He rubbed the back of his hand across his cheeks to remove the tears.

I said, "There are several options to be considered: One, we call the police right here and now. Two, you go home immediately and tell your parents. Three, you can return these pants to the store. Which one will it be, John?"

"Bernie, I thought you would take them back to the store," he said softly, as he moved the pants in my direction.

"John, you have to pick one of the three options I offer. Of course, you may be able to think of another more acceptable alternative. What will it be?"

"Take them back. But will you come to the store with me? Oh, please, Bernie?" he pleaded.

"That's not a problem. When do we do it, John?"

"Next week, maybe?" he questioned.

"Oh no, John, it has to be this week."

"Then, how about Thursday after school?"

"Fine, I will see you here Thursday at 4:30 p.m., John. You must realize that if you are late, I will have no option but to call the police. Is that understood, my friend?"

"Yes, Bernie." The colour was returning to his face.

"Do you understand why I would have to involve the police?"

"No. Not really," the boy replied, as he attempted to wipe a new wave of tears that flowed down his cheeks.

"Well, John, if I take no action in this matter, I will become what is known as 'an accessory after the fact' and could be brought before the courts. It would be as if I had been in the store and helped you steal those pants."

"I see, Bernie. Thanks for this. I . . . uh . . ." His voice trailed off.

"That's okay, John, I appreciate the fact that you had the guts to come in here and take responsibility for your action. I know you will be here Thursday at 4:30 p.m. In the meantime, I will keep these items in safekeeping," I advised, taking hold of the package.

John rose from his chair and extended his hand. "I will see you Thursday, Bernie." We shook hands.

In the meantime I contacted the owner of the store. He was an alumnus of the Boys and Girls Club. In fact, his father had been a member with the Club's founder, Fred C. McCann, back in the 1930s.

I explained the situation about John and that he had volunteered to return the pants. Care was taken not to provide the storeowner with any hints as to how he might deal with the boy.

"You have the boy come in and ask for me. It is the store policy to call the police. However, given the boy's action in approaching you, I will deal with this matter myself," the owner advised.

John showed up at my office at the appointed time on Thursday.

"John, do I understand that you still wish me to take you to the store?" I asked formally.

"Yes. Yes, please," the boy responded.

"Okay. Then you carry the package and let's take my car."

As we drove to the clothing store John said, "I intend to take the pants into the store and apologize. What do you think, Bernie?"

"Sounds okay to me, John. You should realize that this store manager could call the police. Charges could be laid and, if you are found guilty, you will have a criminal record that could dog you for the rest of your life. That is the risk you are taking."

"I know. I . . . I just shouldn't have taken them," he said as if talking to himself.

"John. Let us get one thing straight between you, the store manager, and me. You did not take or rip off those pants. You *stole* them. Understand the point I am trying to make, young man?"

"Yes. And I'm sorry about that," John said.

After parking the car we proceeded to the store. I opened the door and John stepped inside. I then closed the door with me on the outside and John on the inside of the store.

I had fulfilled my part of our arrangement "to take John to the store."

When John realized he was alone in the store, he gave me a forlorn look.

The storeowner caught John's attention. I saw the pants being handed over. Then both of them went to the office in the rear of the store.

About twenty minutes later, John joined me on the sidewalk. He said nothing as we headed to the car.

I took the long route back. "I want to thank you, Bernie," John said as we came within sight of the clubhouse.

"For what?"

"The manager is not going to lay charges," John reported, with a sense of relief.

"Oh, is that so. Did he say why?"

"He told me that when he was a kid he went to the Boys Club and that Mr Fred McCann was so good to him as a kid. The store manager said he knows you. He liked the idea of me bringing the pants back myself. They will not lay charges, this time." The boy extended his right hand in a gesture of gratitude. "Thanks."

"How did you feel when I stayed outside the store?" I asked.

"Oh, I was scared, real scared," the boy replied.

"John, I kept my part of the deal. I took you to the store. There was no suggestion that I was to go into that store with you," I explained with a smile. "So, the next time you make arrangements with someone in authority, make sure you understand what they mean to do."

"Yes. I know that now. By the way, Bernie, how come you knew I wouldn't screw up?" John asked with a smile.

"John, after the way you dealt with me a couple of days ago, I just knew you could handle the situation with the clothing store owner. Anyway, I was just on the other side of a sheet of glass if you or the manager needed me. You should be pleased with the way you handled this whole situation. I am really touched that you could trust me to assist you resolve this matter."

"I sure learned my lesson. Thanks, Bernie," the teenager said.

"Now the challenge that faces you is for you to keep your hands off of other people's stuff. Okay, buddy?"

"It's a deal," John said as he shook my hand before we left the car and got caught up in the activities of the Centre Town Clubhouse.

Commentary:

- It has been my experience that by encouraging children and youth during their formative years to confront the victims of their wrongdoing, it assists in modifying their behaviour and they become contributing citizens.

- Similar situations have occurred over my forty years of youth work. Of all the methods I have used, having young people take back the stolen items to the victim has proven to be most effective.

- By insisting that youth face the reality of their actions—that they *stole* items, not "took them" or "ripped them off"—has proven to be crucial.

- Wrongdoers need to learn that they cannot wish away their negative actions; they have to be encouraged to come forward to resolve errors.

- Providing options to resolve such situations or having the youngsters offer their own acceptable alternatives has proven to have positive immediate and long-term effects.

- Children and youth need to learn that they must tell themselves the truth before they can be expected to be truthful to others.

- Leaders need to learn that regardless of how much we care for our young charges, we cannot live their lives for them.

- Society, family, school, neighbours, and friends provide youth with sets of values and assurances that can resolve difficulties and curb anti-social behaviour.

A VERY ANGRY YOUNG MAN

The sound of raised and angry voices could be heard through the open door of my office. It was apparent that the raised voices came from the second floor of the clubhouse.

As I listened for a few moments, it became evident that one of the voices was becoming shrill.

Arriving in the hallway of the second floor I found Phil with a pool cue in his hand. He was trying to get past Carl, the senior games-room supervisor, who was using his body to shield Vinny from Phil's wrath.

"He's a [bleeping] cheat. [Bleep], that's all Vinny is . . ." Phil sputtered as he waved the pool cue in the air.

"Hey . . . ! Watch your mouth," I demanded, approaching the altercation.

Given that I had not ever seen Phil acting out in this manner during his involvement in Club activities in over seven years, I was puzzled as to what had triggered this conflict.

"What's this all about?" I asked Carl.

Phil spoke up: "Bernie! Vinny *cheated* me in the game we just played. He also lied about the amount of time we had on the table, which Carl now expects me to pay for," explained Phil, as he turned in my direction.

"Excuse me? I asked Carl."

Carl's hand gesture indicated that he did not know the cause of this disturbance.

"Calm down, Phil!" I demanded. "And please place the butt end of that cue on the floor immediately."

"Why should I?" he countered.

"Because that's where it belongs," I responded with a smile.

Phil arched his eyebrows, and lowered the cue as requested.

"What's up, Carl?"

"I really don't know, Bernie. I was on the phone, and when I looked up I saw Phil taking a swing at Vinny with the pool cue."

"I *told* you guys. He was [bleeping] cheating—"

"Excuse me, Phil," I interjected, raising the palm of my hand in his direction. "I'm listening to Carl. Okay?"

The teenager muttered a comment that was not audible so I chose not to pursue it for the time being.

"Phil came very close to cracking Vinny on the side of his head. When I stepped in between them, Phil took a swing at me," Carl reported as he licked his dry lips.

"Oh, yeah . . . Did I hit you?" Phil snarled.

"That's not the point, Phil. The point is that you tried to assault Vinny—and Carl . . . and for what?"

"I told you, Bernie. He cheats." Phil motioned in Vinny's direction.

"If that is the truth, then let the Club staff deal with him. It's not a good reason to hit Vinny and incur a criminal record for assault. Is it, Phil?"

"I didn't hit Vinny," Phil hissed through clenched teeth.

"Sorry, Phil. *Try* to hit Vinny."

Throughout this encounter Vinny had wisely remained unobtrusive.

"I won't miss next time," Phil countered menacingly, as he fixed his narrowing eyes on me.

Placing my hands on my hips, so they were within clear sight of everyone, I decided to turn my undivided attention to the challenge that the Club's intermediate pool and billiard champion posed.

With eyes fixed on Phil, I said, "Carl. Get Vinny out of here."

Phil reacted by taking a step sideways, which I matched. His two quick steps in the opposite direction were also countered.

"Vinny. When will you be here next?"

"Oh. Tomorrow after school . . . I guess?" he replied.

"Be sure you stop by my office. Do you understand?" I stole a quick glance over my shoulder, in his direction, as I spoke.

"Yeah!" Vinny exclaimed as he retreated down the stairs two at a time.

Returning my attention to Phil, I discovered he was moving to the right. My reflex action was to extend both my arms to act as a barrier. In that instant my right arm brushed against Phil's arm.

"Hey! Watch it! You just hit me," he snapped.

I was also aware that he was now tapping the butt end of his pool cue on the palm of his left hand.

"I beg your pardon?" was my immediate response. "And what did I tell you about the pool cue?" I nodded at his left hand.

"You let that [bleeping] cheat go," he gestured towards the stairwell with the cue.

"Watch what you say, Phil. I will deal with Vinny tomorrow. Now if you don't stop swinging the pool cue I will have to remove it." I was attempting to deflect Phil's attention from Vinny and focus on his present predicament.

"I would like to see you try."

"Try what?"

"Try to take this cue from me," Phil challenged, as he held the cue across his chest in both hands.

Taking two small steps backward, Phil extended his arms forward, as if to cross check me with the cue.

"Carl. Did you see that?"

There was no reply. Taking a quick glance behind me, I discovered I was alone with this very angry young man.

Taking one step forward I closed the gap. His reflex action was to take another backward step, while waving the pool cue between us as if it were a car windshield wiper.

"Don't make me . . . " he said, as he bit his lower lip. His eyes were glistening and he was trembling.

"Phil. I don't intend to make you do anything, other than to stop waving that pool cue between us," I countered softly.

"I would like to see you try to take it from me!"

We had maintained eye contact throughout these moves and counter-moves. Phil took two more steps backwards, only to find that the wall blocked any further retreat. His eyes darted from side to side.

"I have no intention to taking the cue from you, Phil. It's your property; and you have not hit anyone, or anything, other than some pool balls. Is that correct?" I smiled.

"Yeah . . ." he sighed as his body went limp.

"I beg your pardon, Phil. 'Yeah'? What's that?"

"Yes, Bernie," was his mocking reply, with a smile.

"Phil, you are too skilled a pool player for most people, including me. Players such as Vinny feel the only way to even the odds against a Club champion, such as you, is to take some short cuts."

"Cheat! You mean *cheat*, Bernie," Phil asserted, placing the butt of his pool cue on the floor.

"You're right, Phil. They cheat." Motioning in the direction of the stairwell I added, "Let's go to my office and figure out what you should do if Vinny, or others, try to cheat you. Okay?"

"Bernie! Bernie. Oh, there you are!" Carl called as he came around the corner from the games room.

"Phil's dad telephoned to say supper was ready. When I told Mr. Watson about Phil's confrontation with Vinny, he said he would be right over."

Phil stopped in his tracks. " What . . . !" the fourteen-year-old boy hissed in disbelief. If looks could kill Carl would have dropped dead.

"Christ. He's going to kill me this time," the boy exclaimed as we proceeded to my office.

Sitting at the table Phil unscrewed the sections of his pool cue. He was having difficulty focusing as his eyes filled with tears.

"I take it your dad is pretty strict, Phil?"

He nodded his head. "Tell me about it. Ever since my mother died he's . . ." his voice dropped off as this young man wiped away tears with the sleeve of his shirt. His Adam's apple danced in nervous anticipation of his father's arrival.

"Do you have other family at home?"

"No." He gave a big sigh, adding, " My Aunt Mary—she is Dad's sister— she and her family live a block away." Tears now streamed down Phil's face.

"Why are you so upset that your dad is coming over?"

"He really let me have it the last time I got into a fight at school. He will also ground me for a very long time." The boy seemed to be talking more to himself than to me.

"Phil, I am very sorry about this. It was too bad your dad telephoned before we had resolved this matter. Carl was only trying to explain your delay, rather than trying to get you in trouble."

He did not react.

"We have a standard rule of informing parents whenever Club members get into fights. Just in case medical treatment is needed, or charges are lodged with the police by the parents of the other fighter."

"But I did not hit anyone." Phil sniffled deeply.

"You know that. I know that. But your dad doesn't know that. So we can confront him together. Okay?"

"Guess so," he nodded.

"Now. Pepsi or ginger ale, buddy?" I headed for the office door.

"Don't care," my guest replied as he rubbed his eyes with the heel of his hands.

Upon returning with the drinks, I saw that Phil had regained his composure. "Here, let's pretend we are both members of the 'Pepsi Generation,'" I joked, sliding a cold canned drink along the length of the table.

"Great! Thanks." He flashed me a weak smile. "By the way, Bernie, you are the only one of us who has to pretend," he added gruffly.

"I walked into that one!" We both shared a laugh at my expense as we started our drinks.

"Now, Phil, what do you want me to do or say when your dad comes?"

"There's not much you can do. You could tell him . . ." his voice trailed away as we both heard a man's voice coming from the front hall.

Phil sank down in his chair.

"In here, Mr. Watson. Hello. I'm Bernie Muzeen." I greeted Phil's father with a handshake at the office door.

I positioned myself in such a way that the worktable stood between father and son.

"What have you been up to now?" he growled. " Why can't—"

"Vinny was cheating, Dad," Phil stated, cutting his father off in mid-sentence.

"But that gives you no cause for fighting. You know what I expect! Come on, boy, let's go home," Mr. Watson demanded.

"Dad, you don't understand. I . . . er—" the boy turned in my direction.

"We can talk about it at home," the man replied.

The ashen face and tear-filled eyes of my young charge moved me to intercede on his behalf.

"Excuse me, please. Mr. Watson, it's true that Phil did become a little angry because Vinny cheated, but he did not get into a fight. Phil never hit anyone. True, he said a couple of things he now regrets, but he did not touch anyone." I emphasized in an even tone of voice, pointing to a chair.

"Yeah. But what about the pool cue?" he asked as he sat down. "I understand from the feller who answered the phone that Phil had—"

"I'm sorry to butt in again, Mr. Watson. I can only guess that the way Phil was swinging his pool cue around gave Carl cause for concern."

I took a deep breath and stole a quick glance at the teenager. He seemed to be hanging on my every word.

"Phil did have several opportunities to connect if he'd wanted. But to his credit your son did not sucker punch Vinny or the Club staff."

The boy gave me a weak smile then cast his eyes down to the tabletop.

"Phil and Vinny are to report back to my office tomorrow, after school. Isn't that correct, Phil?"

"You see, Dad! As Bernie said, Vinny and me have to come here tomorrow," said Phil, making a hand gesture in the direction of his father.

"Son, you'll come right home after school tomorrow, is that clear?" Mr. Watson stated as he stood up.

"Mr. Watson. Would you please let me try to resolve this conflict between Vinny and your son? You see I want Phil to explain to Vinny how really bad it feels to have someone cheat. It's very important for both Vinny and Phil to meet here, with me, tomorrow . . . er, after school."

Mr. Watson was unresponsive. Phil shrugged his shoulders.

"You know, Mr. Watson, you should be proud of the fact that Phil did not hit or punch anyone when provoked. True, he lost his temper—we all do at times—and said things in the heat of the moment. But who doesn't on occasion?" I asked.

"What do you say, son?"

"Dad, I would like to come here tomorrow, after school, and clear it up with Bernie. Okay?"

The man waved his right hand in the air and headed for the door.

"Mr. Watson, thank you for coming over to help. Please feel free to drop in at the clubhouse any time."

He turned and shook my hand and smiled, finally. I said, "There is no reason for us to suspend Phil from the Club, or for grounding him at home, is there Mr. Watson?"

"Sounds fair," Mr. Watson uttered as he walked out of my office.

"Phil, I'm very pleased with the way you handled yourself. You resisted the temptation to take a swing at Carl or me. That's a good first step in learning to control your temper with cheats like Vinny," I assured the teenager.

Phil stood up and walked towards the door. He was nodding his head in silent agreement.

"Come on, son. Dinner's ready," Phil's father stated.

"Your dad's concern is that you could get seriously hurt in a fight. Do you understand, Phil?"

"Yeah!"

"I beg your pardon!" I snapped.

"Yes, Bernie." He had a bright smile lighting up his face.

"Phil, I have an old saying about fighting: 'It's better to be a live chicken than a dead duck.' Think about it!"

"Oh, yes!" he said, rolling his eyes.

"Let's go home, son."

"Dad, can I come back to the Club tomorrow for that meeting with Vinny and Bernie?"

"That's up to Bernie."

Patting me on the shoulder, Phil whispered, "Thanks, Bernie."

Moments later I glanced out the window to see the father gently resting his hand on his son's shoulder as they walked to their car.

Commentary:

- Clearly father and son were grieving their recent loss of a wife and a mother.
- By communicating that verbal abuse was unacceptable, leaders clearly underscore that any attempt to escalate to physical abuse will not be tolerated.
- Insisting that the aggrieved person control his verbal protestations often enables him to "regain hold of reality" as the first step in resolving his perceived conflict.
- Verbal or physical abuse is unacceptable behaviour.
- Both protagonists returned the next day and participated in a reconciliation process.
- Phil became an accomplished adult competitor in the pool and billiard facilities.

THERE'S FOAM EVERYWHERE!

"Chris! What's that stuff you're tracking all over the place?"

"I don't know. But it's all over . . . down there." The seven-year-old pointed in the direction of the stairwell.

"Looks like soap suds," remarked Kyle, a long-time member of the Boys and Girls Club.

"Kyle, please ask the locker room attendant to go down and check on the equipment in the laundry room." I picked up the ringing telephone.

In an effort to answer the questions of the caller I was required to turn around and refer to the list of activities posted on a notice board. In so doing my back was towards the stairwell.

"Oh my Lord! Bernie! You had better see this . . ." Kyle exclaimed moments before I hung up the telephone receiver.

Turning around, there stood Tim and Mark. Legs, chest, arms and hair were covered in white foam. My first reaction was to smile, which these two and Chris returned.

"Trevor did it," Mark stated as his companions nodded their heads in agreement.

"Trevor did what?"

"Bernie, you know the silver thing down there. Well he made all this stuff come out of it," Chris volunteered, brushing foam of his arm.

"Holy cow! There's foam everywhere!" Kyle shouted as he made his way to the basement.

"What is it? What's happened?" I asked, leaning over the handrail of the first-floor landing.

"Bernie, they opened up a fire extinguisher. There's foam everywhere: the walls, ceiling, lights, doors and floor. Oh my Lord, what a mess!" he exclaimed.

"It was Trevor, honest!" Mark said.

"That big guy." Chris raised a hand in the air as if to indicate the other boy's height.

"And where is Trevor?" I asked.

"Don't know," one of the other boys replied.

"He's still down there," whispered Mark.

Just at that moment the locker room attendant, Billy, arrived with a batch of towels and swim shorts to be washed. His first reaction was the same as mine— he smiled.

"What have they been up to?" he asked me.

"I will let them tell you. Please take them to the locker room and clean them up. It's important to be careful that none of that foam gets into their eyes, then have them report to my office by the time I get back."

Joining Kyle in the basement of the clubhouse I observed that his description of the extent of the damage was somewhat overstated. Foam had run down the walls to form puddles in a number of places along the corridor. The sound of running water came from the boys' washroom.

"Trevor. Get out here," I called.

The sound of running water ceased.

I restrained Kyle as he moved in the direction of the washroom.

Several minutes elapsed without hearing a sound.

"Trevor?"

"What!" snarled a thirteen-year-old, stepping into the hallway and adopting the "gunslinger" pose.

I did not respond.

"Yeah! What do you want?" he asked, standing his ground.

"To have you help clean up this mess. I will have the other guys come down here to assist you."

"Bernie! You're wanted on the telephone," someone yelled down the stairwell, disrupting my comments.

"Kyle, will you take charge . . . I'll return as soon as I can."

"No problem."

"Here is the key to the custodian's equipment room. Thanks."

"That's okay," Kyle assured me.

"By the way, I will send those other three down. Be sure that each one does some of the cleaning up," I instructed while heading upstairs.

I found the three boys where I had left them. "Chris, Tim and—" I hesitated, pointing at the third boy.

"Mark!" he exclaimed helpfully, arching an eyebrow.

"Yes. The three of you had better get downstairs and help Trevor and Kyle clean up that mess."

The telephone conversation was unexpectedly lengthy. When I hung up, Kyle was standing at the door of my office with Trevor.

"Kyle. How did it go down there?"

"Fine. Except for this guy. He refused to do any of the cleanup," Kyle said, tilting his head towards Trevor.

"I trust that you and the other fellows didn't do all the work."

"No, Bernie. We left one section for him to do."

"Trevor, you had better get down there and clean it up."

"Or?" he spat defiantly, eyes narrowing in his ashen face.

"What do you mean 'OR,' young man?" I demanded.

"Excuse me, Bernie," the front desk clerk said, knocking gently on the door frame.

"Yes, Harry?"

"It's eight o'clock. These three young lads—" the boys stepped forward, "—want to know if they can go home? They're all juniors."

"Thanks. Now, Tim, Chris, and—" I cleared my throat.

"Mark!" the third boy offered, with a bright smile.

"—Mark, thank you. Did you help clean up?"

"Yes, Bernie." They replied in unison.

"Do you now realize that playing with a fire extinguisher can endanger the safety of a lot of people?"

They nodded their heads.

"Now. Do I need to telephone your parents?"

"No sir," Mark replied.

"Then if there is no need for *me* to tell your parents, I guess there is no need for *you* to have to tell your parents."

"Oh, Bernie!" exclaimed Chris as he impulsively hugged my arm.

"Now get out of here. Go home. Your mothers love you," I smiled.

"Good night, Bernie. Thanks." They scampered towards the front door and home.

"Good night, boys. See you tomorrow."

"Sit down, please" I said, turning to Kyle and Trevor and gesturing with my hand in the direction of the red leather chairs surrounding the worktable in my office.

"Would anyone like a drink?"

"Oh sure! Please," Kyle replied.

Trevor made no comment.

Returning with the membership register and just two canned drinks, I gave one to Kyle and opened the other and started to drink it myself.

"Trevor. Do you realize you have endangered the lives of everyone in the clubhouse by your actions downstairs?"

"Oh, sure!" He folded his arms across his chest and leaned back on the rear legs of his chair.

"Sure you have. In places such as the Boys and Girls Club we are obliged by law to have a certain amount of safety equipment and first aid kits available and in good order at all times. Otherwise we will not be permitted to operate. Luckily for you, and everyone else, we have two spare fire extinguishers. Otherwise I would have to ring the bell and close the clubhouse."

"So?" he shrugged his shoulders.

"SO! When members and their parents ask why, I will have to tell them that Trevor forced us to close the clubhouse."

"Yeah . . . !" he exclaimed with a sneer.

"It may have to be reported to the fire department . . . your school . . . the community arena . . . the library . . . plus any other community facilities you frequent. This is very serious stuff, Trevor."

"We were only having a bit of fun," he pouted.

"FUN! Trevor, you had better—" I took a sip of my drink in an attempt to stay calm. I wanted to be careful not to allow myself to be provoked by this defiant young man.

Trevor closed his eyes as if to make this affair go away. However, his dancing Adam's apple, flushed cheeks and heavy breathing indicated that he had obtained an insight into the gravity of his actions.

"No one got hurt . . . Did they?" he asked softly.

"That's correct, Trevor. But can you be trusted not to interfere with fire safety, alarms and life-saving equipment in other places?"

There was no response. Trevor did place his elbows on the table and bury his face in his hands.

"Trevor, this is the first time in fourteen years that anyone has set off a fire extinguisher."

"Okay. Okay! What do you want me to do?" he asked waving his hands in the air before placing them momentarily over his ears.

"Go downstairs and finish cleaning up the mess you created."

"If I don't?" He folded his arms once more across his chest.

"Then I will have to do three things. The first one is to call your mother to come in and clean up after you, sir."

"No, you can't. She's working," he boasted in Kyle's direction.

"Trevor, just do as he says," Kyle advised softly.

"He can't get my mother in here—"

"Oh, yes I can," cutting short his reply by dropping the membership register on the table in front of this defiant teenager.

Opening the document I looked for Trevor's registration data, while reaching for the telephone.

"Here it is . . . your mother's work number." Peering over the top of my glasses at the young man across the table, I picked up the receiver and started to dial the number.

"But you'll get her fired." His hand moved towards the telephone.

"If your mother gets fired, that's your fault, not mine."

"What do you want me to do?"

"You already refused to do what I asked. I have no—"

"Please, Bernie. Please! Let me have another chance." A single tear ran down his flushed cheeks.

I hung up after dialling five of the required seven numbers. Several moments passed without comment by anyone.

"Finished your drink, Kyle?"

"Yeah . . . er, yes, thanks, Bernie," he smiled.

"Trevor. You asked a few moments ago 'what do you want me to do,' didn't you?"

He nodded his head.

"Before repeating it, let me outline the three steps I promise to take if you do not complete the task to my complete satisfaction: One, I will call your mother to come in from work to clean up your mess; two, I will close the clubhouse for the balance of this evening; three, I will report your action to the fire inspector's office.

"Do you understand that I will do exactly what I've just stated?"

"Yes, Bernie." He let out a great sigh of relief.

"Trevor, I want you to leave this office and go downstairs and finish cleaning up that mess on your own. Do you understand and accept the assignment?"

"Yes."

"How long will it take to finish that task?" I asked, glancing at the clock on my desk

"Oh, about ten minutes."

"And if it's not to my liking . . . ?"

"You will call my mother in to do it." He bit his lower lip.

"Then don't just sit there, man—the clock is running."

Trevor scrambled out of his chair and disappeared into the basement.

"Wow! That was dramatic," Kyle observed, throwing his drink can into the recycle container.

I said, "All too often adults fail to exercise their authority in creative terms when they are confronted with an outright act of defiance."

"By the way, Bernie, it's going to take a lot more than ten minutes for Trevor to clean up down there," Kyle offered.

"So?"

"Will you really call his mother?"

" How much time do you think it will require?"

"Oh . . . about twenty minutes."

"Kyle, will you please turn the hands of the clock on my desk back by twenty minutes?"

"Now that's a neat move!" he exclaimed, picking up the clock. "Bernie, what would the fire inspector do?" he asked, adjusting the clock on my desk.

"I have not the foggiest notion. But then neither does Trevor."

"Really?"

"It could be the fear of two consequences: Those of his mother's, of which he's fully aware; or the unknown one of the fire inspector. In fact, Kyle, I have no idea what action the fire department would take if such a report were made."

"Wow!" Kyle exclaimed.

"Maybe—just maybe—the compassionate manner in which I dealt with the three younger boys inspired Trevor to co-operate. We may never know for sure."

"Calling his mother I understand; but the fire department?" Kyle shook his head.

"Last week our clubhouse underwent a fire safety inspection. Maybe that explains why the suggestion of reporting this matter to the fire inspector popped into my head."

A very sombre Trevor returned to the office fifteen minutes later.

"It's finished." Glancing at his watch he added, licking his lips nervously, "Sorry it took longer than I thought!"

"The timing seems fine according to the clock on my desk," was my response following a careful review of that particular timepiece.

Trevor lifted and crossed arms against his chest, with both hands resting on his shoulders, in the form of a self-embrace. Now he smiled in my direction for the first time throughout this encounter.

"What have you learned this evening, my friend?"

"Not to touch safety stuff. That you will call my mother and er . . . all that stuff you said . . ." his voice trailed off.

"You also discovered that you will be held responsible whenever you make a mistake. And that when given a chance to correct a mistake you have the courage to do it. In that way people will learn to respect and trust you."

"Yeah." Trevor sighed.

"Did you do a good cleanup job in the basement?"

"Oh yes, Bernie. Do you want me to show you?"

"No thanks, Trevor. I'm going to trust that you did a good job."

"Gee! Thanks, Bernie."

"A final thought, my friend. The next time we have a problem, let's work together to resolve it. Okay?" I said, extending my right hand.

"Okay!" Trevor gave me a firm handshake.

Commentary:

- Accepting Trevor's assurance, without reservation, that he had cleaned up the mess was a first step in building a relationship of mutual respect and trust that lasted for many years.

- "Reconciliation and dismissal" for the three young boys may have influenced Trevor to co-operate.
- Leaders need to understand the power of self-redemption for those entrusted to their care.
- Self-redemption is a powerful force in learning to be true to oneself.
- Self-redemption enables those ostracized to correct a wrong and thereby regain trust and acceptance.
- Leaders need to spell out the consequences should one of their charges decide not to correct a wrong.

HAND IN GLOVE

When the six boys in this anecdote arrived at the Centre Town Clubhouse on the Saturday in question, there was nothing in particular that made them stand out from the other youngsters on the bus.

We were delighted to see each other. All became engrossed in the multiplicity of activities offered by the clubhouse. Towards the end of this particular morning, I visited the gymnasium to take in an exciting Cosom hockey game.

"Hi, Bernie," called Jim as he ran past me waving a gloved hand.

"Our team's winning!" Billy yelled as he pointed to the scoreboard with a gloved hand. Moments later, another goal was scored. There was a mixed reaction from those seated in the bleachers.

"That ref stinks," hollered Tom, as he returned to the losing team's bench, his gloved hand waving a hockey stick in the direction of the referee.

Then it struck me. Billy and the other boys were not sporting these very distinctive blue and white leather gloves when they arrived on the bus this morning.

During a break between the second and third periods I gave Jim the "come hither" sign from the doorway of my office.

"A good game?" I asked.

"Yeah. I scored two goals and had one assist," he boasted, as I closed the door behind him.

"Must be the gloves," I observed.

"Oh yeah. I guess so," he responded, averting his eyes from mine, to the blue and white gloves on his hands.

Our eyes caught and locked, as they had so many times over the six years that we had known each other.

Neither of us made a comment or moved for a full fifteen seconds. His blue eyes seemed to be searching my face for a reaction. Then with a wan smile he turned to leave the office.

"Where did you get them?" I asked softly.

Jim stopped in mid-stride. His shoulders slumped and head dropped. He turned back towards me very slowly.

"Come and sit here for a moment," I said, as I pulled a red leather chair from the worktable. However, Jim remained standing.

When I sat down our eyes were at the same level.

"Now, come. Where did you get those gloves, my friend? Before you say anything, remember we have a five- or six-year friendship. I know I can trust you, Jim. I can trust you to tell me the truth the first time."

His downcast head nodded several times.

The distant blowing of a whistle from the gym seemed to snap the boy back to the reality of my office.

He looked at me. A tear had escaped his left eye and was running down his cheek. His lips moved but no words would come out.

"Jim! Jim! Anyone seen Jim?" was the call of his teammate from the hallway.

"We took them," Jim said softly.

"Jim, I am only interested in what *you* did. Not others, just you. Where did you get those gloves?" I asked firmly.

"We went to . . . I mean I went to the store and took them."

"Which store?"

"The Canadian Tire store."

"Which Canadian Tire store?"

"The one over there," Jim said as he gestured with his gloved hand in the direction of Kent Street and Laurier Avenue.

"Why?" I asked.

He shook his head while he wiped away the tears that now rolled down his face.

"Why, my young friend. Why? I would like to understand!"

"I don't know," was the boy's response.

"You suggest that there were others with you, Jim?"

"Right." He started to peel the gloves from his hands.

"That is an important hockey game for you and your team, eh?"

He nodded his head.

"Then I will let you continue to play, with the gloves, on the condition that you will not tell any of the guys that I know about the gloves. Okay?"

"Okay," Jim agreed.

"Wipe those eyes. Clean your face," I suggested, offering him my handkerchief.

Composure regained, Jim opened the office door. Looking back at me he said, "I won't tell them. But they should not know I told on them. Okay?"

"Don't worry, Jim. Those gloves give each one of them away. We have only talked about you at this point," I assured him.

As the last period of the hockey game finished, I invited Bill, Tom, Marc, Jim, Randy and Kevin to stop by my office for a moment.

"Oh, sure," "Guess so," "You've got it," are examples of the informal responses these unsuspecting youngsters gave.

"Bernie. Can you find better refs?" asked Tom, as the five of them entered my office.

"So the Hawks lost again, eh Tommy?" I replied. "Grab a seat, guys. I have something to discuss with all of you. It may take a few minutes."

Other than Jim the boys played a type of musical chairs around the worktable.

The gloves were still on their hands.

"When I saw you guys arrive at the club this morning, none of you sported or showed off those neat gloves."

All hands disappeared from the top of the table in a flash.

With the exception of Jim, all heads dropped as they avoided eye-to-eye contact.

"Now think about it. I'm going to ask you only once: Where did you get those gloves? Remember, I have already told you that none of you had them when you arrived this morning. They are also not the kind of thing we give away at the Club." I looked at each one of the boys.

"Okay. Tom . . . What have you to say?"

Looking up at me with tear-filled eyes, he could only shake his head wordlessly.

"How about it, Marc . . . ?"

He slumped back in his chair, as if to escape my question.

"So. No one has anything to say? Do you have anything to tell me, Jim?"

"Well . . . we took them," he responded softly.

All heads snapped up. Four sets of eyes were transfixed on Jim as he spoke.

"I mean—I took these," dropping his gloves onto the table in front of me, adding, "from the Canadian Tire Store."

Looking at the gloves carefully I observed to no one in particular, "These are still in nearly new condition. They are not damaged too much. Maybe we can return them."

Tom handed his gloves to me, as his friends removed their gloves.

"Hold it, fellows. I don't want any of your gloves until I know how each one of you got them. Is that clear?" I said, lifting my hand to halt their action.

"We took them," Tom snapped at me.

"Don't get mad at me, young man," I retorted loudly. "What do you mean 'we'? Who are 'we'?"

"These guys," Tom gestured with his head.

"I need names. Who are 'these guys,' Tom?"

"Well there's Randy, Jim, Bill, Marc, Kevin and me—Tom."

"How come you gave me your name last? And by the way, where is Kevin?" I asked, looking around the room.

Alarmed, they looked at each other.

"Jim. Go out there and invite Kevin to join us, please," I instructed. "And don't tell him the reason. Okay?"

"If you say so," Jim said, as he went about his task.

Quickly the other boys handed over their blue and white gloves. Each individual admitted that he took or stole them.

"Let's try something. I am going to give you back these gloves before Kevin comes in. Let's see how Kevin handles this situation. Don't any of you give away the fact that I know about the gloves. Okay?" I requested.

"Sure," "Okay," they muttered.

"Before Kevin arrives, we need to know how I should handle this situation. We have several options: One, call the police; two, call your parents; three, take you all back to the store manager and let him deal with you; four, have Bernie deal with it—"

The opening and closing of the outer office door heralded the arrival of Kevin with Jim. It cut off any further discussion of the proposed options.

"Hi, Kevin. Come right over here and sit down," I said, as I pointed to a chair that I had positioned so that the eight-year-old had his back to the older boys.

"Great set of gloves, Kevin."

"Yeah. I found them on the bus, Bernie," he responded without hesitation.

"Then you should have given them to the bus driver. They could belong to some boy or girl who lost them. Is not that a good idea?"

"I forgot," the child replied.

"Then I cannot understand why you did not hand them in to the front desk, to your coach or even me, once you arrived at the clubhouse."

He cast his eyes down to the floor, his legs swinging, his cheeks becoming flushed.

"Are you thinking of an answer, Kevin?"

His head nodded affirmatively.

"Okay, my young friend—one more time—how did you get those gloves?"

Looking at me with his steady steel-grey eyes, Kevin half-turned to the group of older boys and shouted, "They took them! They gave the gloves to me."

"Kevin . . ." someone hissed.

"Bull!" muttered another.

"You lie," spat an older boy.

Turning back to me the little boy burst into tears. He got out of his chair and threw his left arm around my neck, burying his face into my chest.

"It's okay, Kevin. They are not going to touch you. All you have to do is tell the truth. Who was it?"

"What?" he asked, lifting his head off my chest. Licking his lips and brushing away the tears from his cheeks he asked, "What do you mean, Bernie?"

"Who was the guy that stole those gloves and gave them to you? Was it Marc? Or Jim? Maybe Tom did it? How about Bill? Possibly Randy?"

At the mention of each name he shook his head "no."

"Then who, Kevin. Who took the gloves that are on your hands?"

After a look back at the group of older boys, a glance out of the window, and a detailed examination of his gloves, he looked back at me. "I guess I did," he whispered.

"You only guess. You don't know? You are not sure if you took them? Do I understand you correctly?"

"Yeah," the little boy replied, with a deep sigh.

"Those guys were with you. Maybe they could remind you about what happened," I offered.

"No!" he shouted in my face. "I took them."

"Thank you, Kevin. Thank you for telling me the truth.

"Okay, guys. Which will it be: the police, your parents, the store manager, or my way?" I asked, as I leaned back in my chair.

"What will you do?" Randy inquired.

"Let me put it this way. You each have a good idea of what you can expect from your parents?"

"Right!" "Sure do." "Be grounded," the boys replied.

"The police course of action is predictable. However the store manager or my way, you don't know. So what will it be, to trust in someone you know or someone you don't know?"

"I'll go with you, Bernie," Jim said in a clear, firm voice.

"So will I," said Tom.

"Me, too." "Same here," the others joined in.

"Let's get this straight. There is no backing out. You will go along with whatever way I decide to solve this matter?"

"That's okay, Bernie," Jim's voice rose above the buzz of the others, as they talked in hushed tones.

With the children present, I picked up the telephone and talked to the duty officer of the Youth Section of the police. The boys were hushed, to the point that some held their breath. For it was a moment of truth as to whether they had made the correct choice. That is, to have placed their trust in me, without any "deal making" as to the consequences or outcome.

I introduced myself to the police officer who took my call. When we finished with the pleasant salutations, I explained to the officer the circumstances regarding the gloves. Furthermore, I was able to advise that all the stolen items had been recovered, and that the Club members had surrendered the stolen items voluntarily.

The officer explained that he and his colleagues were unavailable for several hours. He asked if I could "hold onto" the young people concerned?

"Excuse me, fellows. The officer informs me that it will be a couple of hours before he can get here to meet with us. It's now 11:40 a.m. Can we all agree to be back at my office by, say, one p.m.?"

All heads nodded approval.

The time suggested met with the officer's approval. However, should any difficulties arise at his end, it was proposed that two p.m. would be a suitable alternative time to meet.

There were several moments of coughing and throat clearing after I had hung up the telephone.

"Sorry about that, fellers. The police have other concerns on their plate at the present time. The officer I was talking to suggests that he can possibly get here by one p.m., but two p.m. at the latest. He sought and I gave him assurances that all of you will be here, at the clubhouse, when he arrives. Do all of you understand what that means?" I asked firmly.

"Bernie, it means that we cannot take off, right?" Jim stated, more for his friends' benefit than for my information.

"You got it, Jim."

Throughout the remainder of the morning these boys were on their best behaviour.

At 12:45 a.m. all were assembled in my office.

"I expect the officer will want to talk to each and every one of you alone. If he and you agree, I can arrange for John, our individual services coordinator, to sit in on the interview. Okay?"

"Why don't you sit in, Bernie? John knows nothing about this—does he?" asked Tom.

"Come on, guys, smarten up. Of course I had to share the police visit with John. How on earth do you think he would know what is going down? Also, he needs to know in case other Club members bug any of you once the police arrive. The other point to be considered is, 'Have you guys told me the truth?' So the only way to find that out is for you to tell your story to the police and John without my being there. Do you understand?"

Heads nodded in the affirmative.

"Do we have to tell our parents about—?"

The ringing of the telephone cut off Marc's interesting question.

It was the police. They now regretted that it would be at least three p.m. before they could see their way clear to get to the clubhouse. In light of this new information I said I would call the officer back within ten minutes.

"Here is how it is, guys. That was the police. The officer from the Youth Section is sorry to say that it could be as late as three p.m. before he can get here. So that means you all still stay at the club, and continue to co-operate. When the police arrive we will have you meet with the officer according to age—the oldest one first—and so on to the youngest. Understand? Okay, Marc, what's the trouble?" I asked him, as he sobbed softly in his place.

"My mum is going to kill me if I get home late," he responded.

"Seems to me it's too bad you did not think about that earlier in the—"

"Excuse me, Bernie?" Jim said as he lifted his hand to get my attention.

"Yes, Jim. Has it to do with Marc's point?" I insisted.

"I think so. You see all of us, except Randy, have to take the school bus home at 3:15 p.m. Will the police be finished in time, if they don't come until three o'clock? Some of us don't have money for the OC buses," he explained with assurance, as he held firm eye-to-eye contact with me.

"Good point, my young friend. What options do you suggest I give the youth liaison officer? You had better be quick about it, because you all heard me tell the officer that I would phone back in ten minutes. What can I tell him you all agree to? Come on." I pushed.

"Tell him to forget it," Tom said with a chuckle. Everyone smiled at that observation.

Jim said, "If he cannot come this week, can he come back next Saturday? Say eleven a.m. We will all be here."

"Boy, oh boy . . . that's asking a lot of everyone," I responded. "I have to trust that all of you will return to the Club next week; that we ask the police to hold off talking with any of you, or your parents, for a whole week. Even more important, you guys have to trust one another that: One, you will all show up next week; two, that none of you will get into trouble, at least for the next seven days; three, you will keep your lips zipped around home until we can figure out how the police wish to handle it; and four, none of you will go around the schoolyard boasting about this. We will have a few principals upset with some of you," I explained to my young listeners. They nodded their heads in unison.

I continued, "The key question is: Will each and every one of you be here next week? Can you guys trust each other? That is the point at issue here. Well, talk it over while I go and get myself a cold drink," I advised, as I headed out the office door.

When I returned in about five minutes, I detected a sense of calm among the boys.

"Bernie, you have our word that we will all be here next week to meet with the police and you, if they cannot make it here by three p.m. today. Right, guys?" Jim said, as he looked around the room to confirm that he had obtained the unanimous agreement of his friends.

"I will see what I can do. And thanks, guys, for trusting each other and me. I will call the officer now and see what I can do. You can stay if you wish or get out there and play."

All the boys opted to stay in my office while I contacted the police officer once more. It became clear that there was a serious doubt that the police would even make it over to the clubhouse today. After assuring the officer that I would put the stolen items in safekeeping, I proposed that he and the boys meet next weekend.

The officer took a moment to consider my offer. The boys, who had by now left their chairs and were gathered around me and the speaker telephone, were holding their collective breath.

The policeman accepted. Once he was given a second reassurance that all the boys would be able to meet with him, he suggested 10:30 a.m. the following Saturday.

"Next Saturday, be here in my office at 10:30 a.m. at the latest. Try to be at the clubhouse about ten minutes earlier, just to be sure we don't keep the police waiting, if they arrive early. Right, fellows?" I asked, as I scanned the faces of this group of relieved boys.

"Thanks, Bernie," was their collective response. One child-sized hand patted my shoulder from behind.

As each of the boys excused himself, I received a number of commitments for their future good behaviour at home, in school and at the clubhouse.

The following Saturday each boy met with a police officer and the coordinator of individual services, to resolve the matter of the stolen gloves. From all accounts these meetings, while necessary, were anticlimactic to the drama of the previous week.

Police Information Reports were made and filed for future reference, by both the police and the Boys and Girls Club.

The children involved learned the value of trust: trust in the police; trust in clubhouse staff; and trust in each other. But most important was self-trust.

This component of self-trust was brought home to me several years later. Jim, who was by then a high school student, dropped by my office for a visit. After some small talk he asked, "Do you remember the time we took some gloves from the Canadian Tire store?"

"Yes, I do. In fact, I never got to tell you how pleased I was with the way you dealt with it, Jim."

"That's okay. Did you know that Kevin nearly screwed it up for all of us that week? He skipped one day of school. I tell you we all kept an eye on each other."

"That's great," was my comment.

"Yeah. But a couple of times when a police cruiser would pass through our housing project we would hold our breath until it had passed on. It was kind of scary—you know, being on edge that one of us might have screwed up."

"Now you see why you were challenged to trust your own behaviour as well as that of each other. Jim, only you guys could do it. You had to realize, once and for all, that you are the master of your own destiny. As much as your mum loves you and I like you, we cannot live your life for you. Only you can do that. Sure, Mum, the school, your church, the Club and even your friends can all share their values. But it is you that chooses which ones to live by. Does that make sense? Excuse me, Jim . . . I did not mean to preach," I offered self-consciously.

"It's okay, Bernie. What you said is right. Those guys . . . well, I learned to trust them and in a way to trust myself," Jim offered.

I nodded my head.

"You know, Bernie, it was real neat to be able to trust someone other than my mum. I was real scared to tell you anything at first. But I am glad I chose to trust you. You know I am real glad that we decided to solve that problem your way. Thanks." Jim got out of his chair and walked towards me with his hand extended. We shook hands and then embraced each other.

Deeply touched by this young man's kind remarks, my eyes became somewhat teary. "I really appreciate your visit and your kind comments. Just know this, Jim, that if you ever need to trust someone in the future, I'm available."

"I know. I know," he said patting me on the back. "Thanks," he said with a broad smile.

"You're welcome, bless you," was my response.

Commentary:

- This encounter with Jim was one of those poignant moments that made me glad I had chosen to be a Boys and Girls Club worker. It is a profession that has provided me with many joyful and satisfactory experiences over a thirty-five-year period.

- I am confident that in turn, Jim will prove to be someone that others can trust—especially in a time of need.

- It also reinforced my confidence in the "preventative guidance value" of the Boys and Girls Club movement. Just where would those children have turned, had a Boys and Girls Club not been a part of their lives?

- Leaders need to encourage "truth telling first time" by those youngsters entrusted to their care and supervision.

- The truth is more effective than one thousand misstatements, lies and falsehoods.

A QUESTION OF HAIR

"Bernie, you once said I could tell you if I had any kind of problem," thirteen-year-old Brian explained. "Well, up to three weeks ago there has been nothing to complain about . . . but lately . . . I'm having a lot of trouble with my parents," the boy said seriously.

Brian took a deep, noisy breath; his eyes were fixed on a spot somewhere on my shirt.

Softly he continued, as if talking to himself. "I want more freedom, but that's something they won't give me. My dad and I keep getting into these fights, about the stupidest things—like me getting my hair cut," he confided.

His hair fell in bangs over his eyes. It also swept from the right side of his head, cascading over his left eye and ear to his shoulder. A bright smile flashed across his face, which became flushed when our eyes met.

"My dad hates it when my hair is falling over one of my eyes. My parents seem to just pick on me. They leave my brother and sister alone. It's not fair!"

"Are you the oldest child, Brian?" I inquired.

"By about five years," he affirmed.

The boy maintained eye contact as he added, "I need some advice from a wise person. Do you know one?" An impish grin lit his upturned face. Then it vanished quickly when he resumed, in a serious tone, "Just joking, Bernie. But we need to talk. Okay?"

"Brian, from what you have told me so far it would seem to be a 'question of hair.' Is that correct?"

"Uh, yeah. It seems to bug him. But after all it is my hair," the boy affirmed.

"True Brian, your hair is yours. You are your own person. However, it is you that has identified that this 'problem' started about three weeks ago. Buddy, I have never met your dad, but I can understand that he would not like you to have long hair. I would guess that it is not the length of your hair that is the issue, per se. He could be embarrassed to be seen with a son who is 'a long-haired kid.' It is your dad's comfort level among his peers and friends that is the issue, given whatever negative connotation of having 'a long-haired kid' might have in his circle of friends. Be they your grandparents, his co-workers, family or acquaintances."

There was a long pause. I noticed a slight nodding of Brian's head, as though he agreed in part with what I had offered for his consideration.

"Your dad may not be unfair. You say that he picks on you, but not your younger brother or sister, Brian. Do they have long hair, eh?"

"No. My parents just pick on me." He placed his head in his hands and his elbows on the table that stood between us. The boy's eyes were half closed.

"Has your relationship with your father been positive, to date?"

"Oh sure. Dad has taken me to all kinds of places. We got on fine, up to about three weeks ago," the boy said, forthrightly.

"Brian. Why let the length of your hair get in the way of the positive and supportive relationship you wish to have with your father? Surely, when you talk about wanting freedom, you should think of issues such as curfews and allowances and friends. Those are the kinds of important things that you and your parents will have to address in the weeks, months and years to come. That's not to say that the style of your hair is not important. However, on balance, are there not more important things in life than the length of your hair?" I let out a deep sigh. "Do you understand the point I am trying to make, Brian?"

"Uh, yeah. I think I do," the boy said, nodding his head.

"As for your brother and sister. Take a moment and recall how you deal with them, when you have to look after them. If you are like me, and others in positions of authority, we set strict rules at first. As those in our care co-operate, we relax the rules and ease off. But when they screw up, particularly if they should know better, we tighten up the rules and start to assert our power, control and authority. Whatever you wish to call it."

The teenager's face was hidden behind a fall of hair.

"In these situations you and I could become bossy, mean, and uncooperative," I explained.

Brian swept the fall of blond hair from off his face.

"My young friend. Just cast your mind back as to how I reacted when you and your friends broke the rules at the Club," I offered.

"I didn't break any Club rules," he said, sorely.

"The point I am trying to make is that I publicly pick on the rule-breakers, be it Paul or Mike, for instance, without letting it affect my relationship with the other members. The effect of publicly going after the nonconformists is, I hope, seen as setting out the acceptable guidelines. Furthermore, my action reinforces acceptable behaviour amongst those within earshot," I explained.

"Uh huh . . ." the boy responded.

"So it may be with your dad, as it relates to your younger brother and sister. As the older child, he could be—rightly or wrongly—using you as an example in setting limits for them. Only you know the truth of that! Anyway, it may not seem to be very clear or fair to you, but that's the way it is with some parents."

"But that's not fair," Brian commented, as he swept the hair from his face once more.

"Remember, Brian, as the oldest child you are in a kind of partnership with Mum and Dad in looking out for and after the well-being of your brother and sister. Is it worth destroying that partnership?"

He dropped his chin to rest on his chest.

"What are your priorities? Of the two of us only you really know what is at stake. You know the kinds of things you wish to do with Mum and Dad. You know them best of all. After all, you have lived with them all your life." We both chuckled at this point. It released the tension of the moment. "Brian, if the length of your hair is your most important desire, for whatever reason, so be it. That's a decision only you can make, my friend."

"Yeah. That about sums it up, Bernie," the youngster sighed.

"One more observation, if I may," I asked, waving both hands in the air.

"Oh sure, feel free," he said, as he mimicked my gesture with both of his hands and a smile.

"Brian, you and your parents are about to embark upon an interesting and challenging time, the teenage years. Is it not better to embark upon this exciting period with an awareness of what bugs and what pleases your parents? The three of you are not always going to agree as to what is acceptable, but that doesn't mean they love you any the less. Think for a moment Brian, you and I both know fellows your age whose parents don't seem to give a damn what they do, what they look like, or where they go. Those young fellows don't seem to have what you have. Think about it."

It was clear that Brian was listening intently to what I was saying.

"The solution to this 'problem' must come from you. Finally, don't expect me to tell you what to do. Brian, know this: Whatever action you take regarding your hair, I will support you and continue to be your friend."

"I'm sure of that. Thanks, Bernie. What you said has been helpful," the teenager said, as he raised his eyebrows in a reaction to some inner thought.

Well, about a week or so later, the telephone rang.

"Guess what I did, Bernie?" Brian asked, following an exchange of greetings.

"Fell off your skateboard and broke your arm?" I enquired.

"No. I got my hair cut, but not too short."

"Is that something you did on your own?"

"Oh, yes," the boy responded.

"How are things at home now?"

"Okay, thanks."

"If you were my son, I would have shaved your whole head. You rotten kid," was my humorous rejoinder.

"Ha . . . ha. I would like to see you try that," he laughed. "I just wanted you to know, and to say thanks for everything," Brian added.

"That's okay, my young friend. Call me again if ever I can be of help or you wish to sound out an idea or two. Brian, thank you for placing your trust in me. God bless and good luck."

I hung up the phone knowing that young Brian had learned an important lesson in compromise, while retaining independent will power and self-confidence.

This was one fellow for whom there was a good chance that he would survive his teenage years in partnership with his parents.

Commentary:

- A good listener, like a good mirror, should truly reflect what is being communicated.

- The listener should heighten distortions, repeat positive conclusions and illuminate unspoken factors.

THE COLOUR OF HIS HAIR!

A group of eleven- to thirteen-year-old boys sought to gain access to the bi-weekly teen dance, sponsored by the Kanata Youth Centre. All had their hair heavily gelled and combed into "spikes," the current fashion.

"Let him get closer . . ." "Come on, make way . . ." "Don't push!" were comments that seemed to be focused on a companion standing across the lobby from me. The boy's hair was dyed bright red with a green streak that ran from the crown of his head to the nape of his neck.

Eventually, the object of their concern had manoeuvred himself so he was standing immediately in front of me. Given the expectant expressions on his companions' faces, they anticipated some kind of reaction from me.

Clearly I was expected to notice the colour of his hair. Inwardly, I resolved to resist making any kind of personal comment.

Nevertheless, the moment of truth came when Mike asked with a sweet smile, "What do you think, Bernie?" inclining his head in the direction of the boy standing immediately in front of me.

"What do I think of what?"

"The hair, man! The hair," he hissed through clenched teeth.

Taking my time I slowly surveyed the hairstyle of each member of the group.

"Well?" Mike exclaimed impatiently.

"You really want to know what I think?"

"What . . ." "Come on!" "Oh, yeah!" were their comments.

"It's remarkable that none of you fellows knows how to comb your hair properly," was my considered reply to the upturned eager young faces.

There was an audible groan from the group as they made their way to the cashier.

"Is that guy blind?" commented the boy with the dyed hair.

During the dance I learned the boy's name was Tom.

Several weeks later, Tom arrived at another dance with his hair dyed green.

"What do you think of this, Bernie?" he demanded, placing his colourful head of green hair within inches of my face.

"Well! As Kermit the Frog said, 'It isn't easy being green!' That is all I can think of right now, Tom."

"Good one, Bernie!" Tom replied, giving me a high-five handclasp.

After several months to grow through this phase, Tom's hair returned to its natural colour.

Given that many adults consider that dyeing their hair is fashionable or makes them look younger, I'm dismayed that when youngsters dye their hair they are often dismissed as "nonconformists." No wonder young people don't know what is really expected of them.

Young people's motivations in dyeing their hair include: a desire to be noticed; the need to be different, to rebel or shock, mimic a singer, an actor, a sports star or other notable; make a fashion statement; fit in with their peers, or to be the "nonconformist" among their peers; or perhaps simply to express an aesthetic appreciation of the colour!

Commentary:

- Accepting Tom as a person—and not reacting negatively to his hair colour—showed personal respect towards him in front of his peer group.
- Such an approach may have been reassuring for Tom while having a positive influence on his peers.
- Leaders need to be circumspect when invited to pass judgment or comment on the personal appearance of others.

PART VI

Bullies

PENALIZING A VERBAL BULLY

"Stupid [bleep], you missed the open goal!" Ralph yelled at a smaller, less coordinated teammate.

"Watch your mouth," the referee cautioned.

"Come on four eyes, pass it," Ralph called to his right-winger as they both closed in on the Hawks goal crease a few minutes later.

"Ralph, smarten up. You're both on the same team," coach Don called out to the Knights' foul-mouthed player.

"What a goof! You just gave the [bleeping] puck away and the Hawks scored!" Ralph berated Chris, the team captain, as they both took their seats on the team bench following a line change.

"Ralph, if you keep up with your offensive remarks I will bench you for the remainder of the game," his coach warned.

"For Chrissake, what did—"

"Shut up, Ralph," the team captain cautioned, cutting him off mid-sentence.

"The Knights can receive a team penalty. You can be kicked out of the game. So watch what you say. I mean it, Ralph!" the coach demanded.

"But what did I say?" he asked, a bewildered expression on his face.

The game went on.

Then Ralph said, "The [bleeping] ref must be blind to miss that call!"

"Quiet!" "Watch it!" "Come off it!" were the frustrated comments made simultaneously by his exasperated teammates.

Too late. The referee blew his whistle and gave a "team misconduct" penalty against the Knights. They had to play for two minutes with one less player than the Hawks, as Ralph sat in the penalty box.

Before the start of the second period of this Cosom hockey game, the referee called the captains and coaches of both teams into the centre of the clubhouse gym.

"The linesmen and scorekeeper agree with me that verbal bullying or intimidation is unacceptable behaviour. Players who make such un-sportsmanlike remarks, be they directed at their own teammates, opponents, or game officials will be penalized," the referee announced.

"Does that mean the Knights will get more 'team misconduct'? You know what Ralph's like," Chris, the Knights' team captain asked.

"No, Chris. It wouldn't be fair to the other players who follow the rules. We will penalize the individual players for their verbal abuse, and any other rule infractions," the referee advised.

"Thanks," sighed Chris.

"Will teams have to play short-handed?" the Knights' coach asked.

"No. Our intention is to penalize any player who swears or voices derogatory remarks. Three infractions will result in that player being suspended from the game."

Team representatives agreed and accepted that the game officials should enforce these rules. Captains and coaches returned to their team benches and explained to their teams the consequences regarding further verbal abuse, bullying or intimidation.

A whistle blast announced the commencement of the game. The play went back and forth between both goals for twelve minutes without any offensive verbal interaction or intimidation between players.

Unfortunately Patrick, with less than two minutes remaining to play, misjudged the puck and ran into his own goalkeeper, allowing the Hawks to score.

"Damn it, four eyes! Watch what you're doing," Ralph exploded.

"Personal misconduct penalty against Ralph," the referee said as he recovered the puck from the goal net.

"What for?" screamed Ralph.

"You don't need me to remind you about the verbal abuse penalty. You're out of the game for two minutes." The official pointed to the chair next to the scorekeeper's table.

"You're [bleeping] crazy! I didn't say anything," Ralph argued.

"Another penalty," a linesman announced, blowing his whistle.

"Penalty! You must be nuts. Don't you guys know that there's less than two [bleeping] minutes to play?" Throwing his stick in the direction of the referee, Ralph stormed out of the gym.

Team members, volunteers and Club staff reported this incident to me in great detail. Clearly this individual was not willing to accept that the comments he was making, in the heat of the game, were offensive. Nor that he was verbally intimidating the players of both teams and the game officials.

An hour or so after this happened, Ralph attempted to enter the gymnasium to play basketball.

"Bernie wants to see you before you're allowed back in our gym," Don informed the fourteen-year-old.

So it was against this background that Ralph and I were brought together.

"Hi! You want to see me?" Ralph stood in the doorway of my office.

"Excuse me! Show some manners and knock on the door, please."

Rolling his eyes the boy rapped on the metal doorframe.

"Please sit down, Ralph. I'll be with you in a minute," I said as I returned to making a notation on a report I had been reading.

"Ralph, do you like coming to the Club?" I inquired.

"Of course. Why do you ask?" a bewildered expression on his face.

"I'm told you were very upset with players, officials, even your team coach and players this morning."

"Oh. Is that why I'm not allowed in the gym?"

"Tell me what happened this morning—"

"Nothing!" he exclaimed.

"—during the Cosom hockey game," I said, finishing my question.

"Oh that . . . They're all goofs, Bernie." He waved an arm dismissively.

"Please tell me about it, as I was not there."

"They are so stupid that they tried to give me six minutes in the penalty box when there was less than two minutes left to play. Those boneheads," he snarled.

Placing both elbows on the table and resting my chin in my hands I looked at the boy without making a comment.

"What?" Ralph demanded throwing open his arms.

"Mmm . . . ! 'Stupid,' 'goofs,' even 'boneheads'!" I repeated.

"Yeah!" the boy grunted.

"Sounds to me like you are a bully—"

"No. I didn't hit anyone," Ralph interrupted.

"A verbal bully . . . verbal intimidator . . . verbal abuser, I should have said."

Ralph remained unresponsive.

"Don't you realize that verbal abuse can hurt deeply, frighten others, foster discrimination, and create emotional distress that in many cases has a more lasting effect than physical abuse?"

Several moments passed without comment.

Finally I said, "I'm not too sure if I would like to hear what you would call them, and me, when you get *really* angry. In fact I have been told that you used a lot stronger more offensive language with the game officials, your coach and even your own teammates. Is that correct?"

"Those Knights deserved to lose. They are no good without me." He seemed to be trying to change the subject under discussion.

"But they didn't lose. Patrick tied the game after you quit. So they seemed to get on quite well without you, my friend."

"Lucky [bleep]," he smiled.

"There you go again. That foul mouth is what got you kicked out of the game."

"I was not 'kicked out.' I quit the stupid game!" He banged his fist on the table that was between us.

"You are out of the gym for the rest of today. Furthermore, if you wish to join in a Cosom hockey game in the future you will have to spend the first six minutes in the penalty box."

"Says who?"

"Says me," I asserted, making a loud cracking noise by bringing the flat of my hand down on the table.

"Oh. You!" the boy responded, a startled look on his face.

"Ralph, your verbal bullying, abuse, intimidation, and bad-mouthing, or whatever you call it, of this morning, plus your bad attitude here in my office seems to indicate you don't like coming to the Club."

"But you're wrong, Bernie. I like it here. Honest!" he exclaimed.

"Wow! Then you need to learn what we have in store for you should you continue to swear at our Club members, volunteers and staff."

"What?" He licked his dry lips.

"Sitting in that chair," I said, pointing to the chair at the end of my worktable, "with me for company. How would you like that, Ralph?"

He raised his eyebrows, took a deep breath and shifted in his chair without further comment.

"So, Ralph, if you cannot control that stream of verbal abuse that pours out of your mouth in the gymnasium, swimming pool, games room, TV lounge, craft shop, fitness centre, kitchen, computer room, locker room, or even on the baseball field, you will be expelled from each of those ten program areas. Consequently, that chair will be the only place you will be permitted to use in this clubhouse. Understand?"

He nodded his head.

"It may seem to be easier for all concerned to just kick you out. But here we resolve problems—not transfer them to the streets."

Ralph remained silent.

"It's not that Club members, volunteers and staff don't like you! It's the verbal abuse we don't appreciate," I added softly.

"But it just comes out. I can't help it! Honest, Bernie."

"You must learn to control each verbal outburst, Ralph. If you do make an offensive comment, an immediate apology may help those you offend not to become too angry towards you."

"But . . . !"

"Ralph, there is no BUT. You know the Knights did not lose after you quit the game. So it will be with lots of other children. They will find ways and means to avoid accepting you as a teammate, or a friend, because they don't appreciate being bullied, verbally, by you."

Nodding his head with closed eyes, I felt that this young man was envisioning a very lonely future.

"Who's in charge?" I asked.

"You are, Bernie," he said, looking up at me with large brown eyes.

I slowly shook my head.

"Oh. It's me."

"That's correct, Ralph. Only you can control what comes out of your mouth. No one else. What's more, I'm not suspending you from our Club. I will just keep this chair ready for you. If that does not work, we have other methods that include your parents, studying a dictionary, and even homework projects to help you break a very bad habit."

"Sorry, Bernie." He extended his right hand.

"That's a good start. But don't forget those people you verbally offended earlier today," I said, grasping his extended hand.

"I won't," he nodded with a smile.

"Also, the six minutes you must serve in the penalty box. Right?"

"Yeah," he muttered. "I mean *yes*, Bernie." Ralph responded immediately to the scowl on my face.

"Go on. Get out of here and be pleasant to people," I said, waving my hand towards the door before returning to the unfinished report on my desk.

Commentary:

- Slowly but surely, with guidance, encouragement and time, Ralph learned to curtail his verbal bullying.

- Verbal abuse, bullying and intimidation can leave serious emotional, racial, and cultural scars on the victims that last a lifetime.

- Leaders must avoid "collective punishment" for the verbal transgressions of a single member. In this situation it was unfair to collectively punish the Knights for the uncontrolled verbal misbehaviour of a single teammate.

- Isolating an offender assists him to comprehend the nature of his unacceptable behaviour as a first step to his social reintegration.

- Failure to assist offenders in controlling and modifying their verbal abusive behaviour would be inhumane.

BULLY IN THE MAKING

In my capacity as a volunteer/chaperon for the Kanata Youth Centre dances, my duties were to monitor the orderly transfer of youngsters from a designated lounge to the gymnasium where a teen dance was being held. Furthermore, along with my colleagues, we tried to forestall any "anti-social behaviour" before it got out of hand.

This is an example of the preventative approach at work.

From my vantage point I observed a fourteen-year-old boy in a white baseball cap move in behind an unsuspecting smaller, younger boy, and shove him with such force that his victim staggered halfway across the lounge.

"That's the kid I'm going to fight tonight!" this 'bully in the making' loudly boasted to his escort, as they turned in my direction.

"Oh, oh! Bernie saw you!" his companion exclaimed as I moved to intercept them in the corridor.

"Let's step into the office," I said sternly to the boy with the white baseball cap.

"I'm not with him," the escort commented as he scurried away, losing himself among the 300 teenagers attending this bi-weekly dance.

"Let us send you home in a police cruiser," was my opening comment as I closed the office door.

"What did I do?" the boy exclaimed.

Turning to my two fellow volunteers who were using the office, I described in detail what I had just observed.

The boy in the white baseball cap exclaimed, "Oh, that kid's a pest. I know . . . uh . . . we go to the same school." He seemed flustered and at a loss for words.

"So? Does that excuse you for what you just did to him?"

"No." The colour drained from his face as his blue eyes locked with mine.

"What's your name?"

"Chris."

"My name's Bernie, Chris. Now tell us what you did?"

"Well. That other kid is a . . ."

"It is what YOU did, young man." I cut off any further commentary about the other boy.

"I pushed him. Like you said." Tears welled up in his eyes.

"And . . . !" I exclaimed.

"Nothing . . . honestly!" Chris licked his lips.

I said to my colleagues, "You had better call this boy's mother, and the police, because Chris has stated that he intends to engage that younger boy in a fight after the dance."

"Oh, *that*! You heard?" said Chris, arching his eyebrows in disbelief.

"Well!" I said, clearing my throat.

"It's true. But I won't do it. Honest!" He directed his comments to the other volunteers in the office.

"Chris, there are three witnesses here who have just heard you admit to assaulting that other boy," Julie, one of the volunteers observed.

"I just shove—I mean—pushed him." Chris demonstrated a hand and arm motion for the benefit of the volunteers.

There was a long pause.

"How can we trust you? Better that you tell that to your mother when she picks you up," I offered on renewing eye contact with the boy.

Turning to the other volunteers Chris pledged, "I promise that I will not hit that kid again, or get into a fight with him after the dance. Please, don't call my mother?" A single tear escaped from his left eye.

"Well, that's up to Bernie!" Julie said.

"Oh. Please, Bernie!" He clasped his hands together. "They can be my witness," Chris added softly, pointing to my fellow volunteers.

"Then get out of here . . . and keep your hands to yourself!" I advised, as I opened the office door.

A look of great relief swept across his face. After taking three steps into the corridor Chris glanced over his right shoulder and whispered, "Thanks."

"Remember, Chris, you personally set the terms and conditions of your behaviour for the remainder of this evening. So enjoy."

"I will, Bernie," he responded with a bright smile.

Later Chris asked me for the time. I said, "Ten-twenty p.m. Everything's okay?"

"Sure, Bernie." He extended his right hand, which I shook, confident that this 'bully in the making' may have learnt a valuable lesson.

Commentary:

- This boy's truth telling was remarkable and had to be acknowledged.
- The survival and self-preservation instincts are a strong impulse in bullies.
- Leaders are encouraged to have bullies take an active part in selecting remedies to modify their behaviour. I'm confident that Chris's self-selected remedy was more effective—even less disruptive—in modifying his immediate and long-term behaviour than any conditions I could have attempted to impose.
- Leaders must assist their young charges to establish terms and parameters that result in behaviour modification.

THE AVENGER

"Jeff is at it again," my secretary remarked, as she ushered a group of youngsters into my office, with seven-year-old Tom. Tom must have been the fifth youngster to have been brought into my office in tears that day.

He exclaims, "Jeff did it!"

I had known Jeff for almost three years as a Club member. He envisioned himself as tough, with a "So what are you going to do about it?" attitude.

Warnings, heart-to-heart talks, suspensions from programs, and other courses of action seemed to have little or no effect on this twelve-year-old boy.

A complaint to his mother, in the past, had backfired. Instead of joining with the Club staff in modifying Jeff's behaviour, Mrs. Jones withheld the boy from the clubhouse for several weeks. Needless to say, upon his return the boy took out his pent-up anger on the members and staff. As a result, the staff undertook to resolve Jeff's conflicts within the clubhouse.

To this end, I came to the conclusion that it was about time for Jeff to participate in "the lineup role-play" in an effort to get an important message across to this strong-willed twelve-year-old.

So it was that the 'lineup' was formed. It consisted of Tom (age nine), Jeff (the bully), then Danny (age fourteen), Chuck (age sixteen), and then Shawn (age seventeen). Each boy was clearly head and shoulders taller than the one to his right.

"Jeff, we are all here to provide you with a very important message. Do you know what it is?" I asked, as I pointed from little Tom to the tall and hefty Shawn.

"Beats me," was his response, as he dug his hands deep into the pockets of his jeans.

"The point is that you cannot go around, here or anywhere else, bullying others. This boy, Tom, must be the fourth or fifth little fellow you have hurt today. Why, Jeff?" I demanded firmly, as I held my face within inches of his.

"He's a wimp."

"Who is he?"

"That guy" Jeff shot back, with a defiant tone to his voice and inclining his head in the direction of Tom.

"What's his name?"

"How do I know?" he spat back, without taking his brown eyes off me.

We glared at each other, each willing the other to speak first.

"Tom, it's Tom," whispered his victim.

"Oh yeah, it's Tom," Jeff sneered, as he shifted his weight from one foot to the other.

I smiled and thought: *we got to him.*

"What's so funny?" Jeff demanded, as he reacted to my smile and brought me back to the business at hand.

"Jeff, what did Tom do?"

"What do you mean?"

"I want to know what Tom did to you to cause you hit him," I asked, with an exasperated sigh.

"I don't know. Nothing, I guess."

"Jeff, do you know why these guys are here?"

"No. But I know that I didn't do anything to any of *them*," he said, as he looked down the line towards Shawn.

"We are all here to teach you a lesson. Now, do I have this right? Tom did nothing to you, Jeff, yet you hit him. Right?"

A nod of the head was his unspoken response.

"Well, Danny is going to hit you. Chuck will hit Danny and Shawn will punch Chuck. Do you understand, Jeff?"

"I guess so," was his dry-mouthed response.

My order, "Okay, Danny, you punch Jeff" brought no reaction from the bully. He just looked ahead. However, the colour drained from his face.

"What was that?" Danny asked.

"Danny, what would you do and say if I told you that you can hit Jeff?"

"Sure thing. I have wanted to hit this sucker for picking on my kid brother at school." With that said, Danny's arm swung through the air, much to my surprise.

Luckily for everyone, I caught a glimpse of Danny's arm cutting through the air. I was able to step forward and block his punch with my chest and shoulder before it could impact on its intended target—Jeff.

"Oh come off it, Bernie, you said I could hit him," Danny protested, with disappointment in his voice.

"I know I did. But it's my job to protect Jeff from you, Danny, even if you think you have good cause to hit this bully. Just as I have to protect Tim, your little brother, and other guys from Jeff," I explained to this would-be avenger.

At this point, a single tear escaped from Jeff's left eye. His dancing Adam's apple was another indication that he was not so tough.

"Clear out of here, everyone except Jeff," I said, as I walked the other boys to the outer door of my office. After thanking them for their co-operation, I returned to my office and sat in the chair next to Jeff.

"Did you really think I would stop him from hitting you?" I asked softly.

"Guess so. Well, yeah," was the boy's reply, as he wiped a couple of tears from his face.

"How come?"

"What do you mean, Bernie?" he asked, a puzzled look on his face.

"How come you figured that I would not let Danny hit you?"

"Because you don't let me hit other kids. When I do, you get real mad," Jeff explained, as he let out a great sigh.

"Then why *do* you hit the younger club members, Jeff?"

"I don't know," he muttered, as he dropped his head.

"Did you really fight or beat up Danny's little brother?"

"He started it at school. Someone phoned my mum about it. I got grounded for a week."

"Did your mother give you any advice?"

"Kind of."

"Well. What was it, Jeff?"

"That I should not get into fights," he shot back.

"So. Your mother, Danny, the Club staff and I—all of us are telling you not to bully the little fellows. Right, Jeff?"

"Right, Bernie." He smiled for the first time.

"I am going to ask for one more thing, my young friend."

"What's that?" he inquired, fixing me with those large brown eyes.

"Stop picking on and hurting younger/smaller children. If you continue, it suggests to me that you, Jeff, are a bully. Just look what it could lead to, my young friend. Older brothers wish to find you and hurt you. Other fellows do not wish to be your friends, in case you beat them up. Little guys will be afraid to play with you. Tell me, Jeff: is it all worth it?"

"No, Bernie," he responded, with another sigh. "I don't mean to hurt those kids. Sometimes we are just playing. I didn't mean to hurt anyone . . ." his voice trailed away.

"I know how you feel, Jeff. I had a similar problem when I was your age," I confessed.

"What's that?" the boy asked, arching his eyebrows.

"I did not realize how strong and powerful I was for my age. Like you, I found I hurt some of the kids I played with. That got me into lots of trouble."

"Yeah. I know what it's like," he responded, nodding his head.

"Jeff, be careful. What you need to do is to make friends. It may be slow and tough at first, but you can do it. If I can ever help, you let me know."

"I know, Bernie."

"By the way Jeff, I have to say sorry, to you."

"To me? Why?" His voice was an octave higher and his eyebrows were arched in surprise.

"Because I did not expect Danny to attempt to hit you. Luckily for all of us I was able to stop him in time. I am really sorry for giving you a scare." I extended my hand.

He shook my hand. "That's okay, Bernie," he said. "Dan did scare me, just a bit," he added, with a shy smile.

"Well, Jeff, he scared me a whole lot more. That punch of his really hurts," I said, rubbing the impact area.

The boy laughed. "It taught you a lesson, eh?"

"Sure. This is the first time the 'lineup' has backfired on me," I complained with a wince.

Both of us looked at each other and smiled broadly.

"This is worth a celebration. The drinks are on me," I said, as I fumbled for the money in my pocket.

"I know . . . I know, a Diet Pepsi for you and whatever I want for me," Jeff said brazenly, as he held out his hand for the money to feed the cold drink dispenser.

Commentary:

- This situation taught me an important lesson. Whenever I ran this role-play thereafter, I would privately coach the individual assigned to stand next to the bully to only *pretend* to hit him!

- Leaders need to be sensitive to a variation of the Golden Rule: "Others do unto me as I do unto them." I have found it to be a powerful, positive and rewarding approach.

- Sad to tell, there are leaders who adopt the old and negative adage, "Do as I say, not as I do." It has been my experience that this attitude leads to puzzlement, confusion, and downright hostility on the part of the victims of this double standard.

HE'S MY FRIEND

Ralph and Randy were inseparable. They were fast friends. This was all the more remarkable given that Ralph was a "hot dog" and an overachiever and Randy seemed to be the tagalong type, an easygoing boy with an outgoing, friendly attitude to one and all.

The two of them played endlessly. The ending of each encounter was predictable. Randy would finish second to Ralph.

The day came when this relationship was to be tested and changed forever.

Ralph was giving Randy a difficult time in the gymnasium. It resulted in raging and roughhousing his friend, with a basketball, beyond the point of endurance.

Randy lashed out in a moment of frustration and pushed his friend in a desperate attempt to get his hands on the basketball.

This unexpected aggressive action caught Ralph off-guard, causing him to fall heavily to the floor. Immediately, Randy rushed over to assist his fallen comrade to his feet. In return for this kindness, Randy received several forceful punches to the face, chest and upper arms. Both boys immediately became entangled as they wrestled each other to the floor.

It took several minutes for the phys ed. staff to disentangle the boys. Once this was accomplished, they were both escorted to my office by a disbelieving staff.

A quick examination of Randy showed several red welts that could turn into major bruises. Ralph seemed to have only bruised his ego.

"Go wash your face and calm down, Randy," I instructed a shaken young man.

"This is a fine mess you have gotten yourself into, Ralph," I informed him, once his friend had left my office.

"I know. He's my best friend," he responded, ruefully.

"What a way to treat a friend. You must have hit him real hard. Randy has received some serious welts and bruises from your fists."

"I know. I didn't mean to . . ." he trailed off, as though at a loss for words.

"You realize that I will have to do something about this?" I asked the fourteen-year-old.

"I guess so . . ."

"When Randy returns to this office I wish to talk to him alone. You will leave my office, close the door behind you and sit on the chair outside, until I call for you. Do you understand?"

"Yes, sir," Ralph replied formally.

"Hi. Can I come in?" Randy asked, as he knocked softly on the office door.

"Come in, Randy. Please sit at the head of the table."

I nodded in Ralph's direction. He stood up. Took a long look at his friend. "I'm sorry. Are you okay?"

"Sure. I'm fine."

Ralph left the office and closed door behind him.

"Ralph's your friend?"

"Sure is."

"For how long?"

"About eight years, I think. Anyway, since we were in grade one."

"This friend of yours. How many times did he hit you today?"

"I don't know," he responded, with a shrug.

"Would you say five or six times?"

"I didn't count," a puzzled expression on his face.

"You like him? Even after what he did today?"

"I guess so. Anyway it was my fault. If I had not pushed him off the basketball, Ralph would not have fallen and been hurt."

"I see. You know that Ralph will have to be punished for what he did to you. You do realize that?"

"Yeah . . . !" he hissed through his teeth. "Like what?"

"Well, if you don't object I could call the police and have assault charges laid."

"No. Not that."

"Then I should call his parents and demand that they come here and take him home, right now."

"I don't think that's such a good idea, Bernie."

"Then Randy, as the victim you will have to help me determine Ralph's punishment. Okay?" I pressed.

"If you say so."

"Ralph! Ralph, get in here," I called.

Once he was in the office I gestured for him to stand to the right of my chair. Ralph took a good look at his friend, seated in the large chair at the other end of the worktable, which stood in the middle of the room.

When he finally turned his attention to me, we established and maintained eye contact. "You will have to be punished for what you did to Randy."

"I know," he sighed.

"How many times did you hit Randy?"

"Five or six times, I think," he responded as he turned towards his friend. It seemed that he was seeking confirmation.

"That is what you are going to get," I snapped.

That comment brought his undivided attention back to me.

Waving my size fifteen hand in front of Ralph "This is what you are going to get, if Randy agrees. He's the victim."

"I know."

"Randy, what do you say? Here's your chance to get back at this bully. Shall I slap him once for every punch he gave you?" I asked, without breaking eye contact with Ralph.

"No. No, don't do that," Randy almost shouted, as he reached along the table, towards me.

"Why not?" I asked abruptly. "This bully boy needs—"

"He's my friend, Bernie. I don't want to see him get hurt," was Randy's response that cut me off in mid-sentence.

Both boys looked at each other. I could detect a slight smile on both their faces.

"Boy oh boy, Ralph, how lucky you are to have a friend like Randy. I sure hope I can find a friend like him. Particularly when I'm in trouble," I said, nodding my head in agreement.

Placing his left forearm on my shoulder, this tough boy turned to me with tears in his eyes. "I know," he choked, as he rubbed the knuckle of the index finger of his right hand, in each eye socket.

"Sorry, Randy. You all right?" he turned and asked his friend again.

"Sure. I'm okay," Randy replied, with a broad smile.

"You two are so very fortunate to have each other as friends. Don't screw it up. Good friends are so hard to find. The next time you have a misunderstanding, you may not be lucky enough to resolve it."

They both stood there looking at me.

"For goodness sake, both of you get out of my face," I said, as each of them gave me the high five.

"Beat you at 'donkey,' Randy," boasted Ralph, as he pushed his way past his friend, as they exited my office.

"Ralph. Get back in here!" I hollered.

He returned to the office, wide-eyed. "What!"

"Let Randy win once in a while," I advised with a wink.

He broke into a broad smile and said, "Sure. Sure thing, and thanks, Bernie," he gave me the thumbs-up sign.

"Ralph, get that basketball," he called to his friend as he hurried after him into the gymnasium.

I am confident that Ralph and Randy have a friendship that will last a lifetime.

Commentary:

- The method outlined in this story has been used repeatedly when attempting to resolve misunderstandings between children who are good friends.

- The result in similar situations, in over forty years of working with children and youth, has not produced a single request for any retaliatory action against the aggressive party.

- It demonstrates to the aggressive parties that their victims envision a positive alternative to physical retribution. It has resulted in a reduction of repeat incidence.

PART VII

Camp Miniwassin

Camp Minwassin, which is owned and operated by the Boys and Girls Club of Ottawa–Carleton, plays a key and supportive role in the provision of preventative guidance and counselling services for some 400 children, eight to fourteen years of age. Each summer, campers are drawn from among the 3,500 members of the Boys and Girls Club of Ottawa–Carleton, and the community at large.

Camp Minwassin is located on a nine-acre site, selected in 1923 by Fred C. McCann, on the sandy shore of Mink Lake, Eganville, Ontario. Since its inception, Camp Minwassin has been a haven for uncounted thousands of children, many of whom come from limited-income, single-parent and multi-problem families.

A ROYAL VISIT

The Buckingham Palace Office of The Prince of Wales informed the Boys and Girls Club, "It's the wish of H.R.H. to experience, as much as possible, a typical day in the life of Camp Minwassin."

The Brian Smith Outdoor Education Centre—formally known as Camp Minwassin and now called "Camp Smithy" by youngsters who use this wonderful natural facility—was the first engagement for H.R.H. The Prince of Wales on the occasion of his first official visit to Canada, in July 1970.

Excited campers gathered on the grass strip between the road and the basketball court, searching the broken rain clouds for a first glimpse of the helicopter that would carry the royal visitor to our camp. The rat-tat-tat of helicopter blades beating against the sky announced the impending arrival of the royal party long before it came into view. One, then two, additional helicopters dramatically appeared above the tree line.

While the first two helicopters landed in the baseball field to allow security personnel, aides from Buckingham Place, representatives of the Canadian government and the media to disembark, the third helicopter, piloted by the Prince of Wales himself, circled overhead. Once all was ready, the royal pilot landed his helicopter in the centre circle of the basketball court.

Campers greeted the prince with a great "Eeeeee . . . POW!" the traditional camp greeting, as he set his foot on the soil of our camp. President A. de L. Panet, Executive Director Richard Wood, and Camp Committee Chairman Fred J. Ellis, accompanied by a camp counsellor and two campers, stepped forward and greeted Prince Charles on the occasion of his first official visit to Canada. Preceded by a security wedge of Mounties, the official party followed a bagpiper to the camp van, which drove them to the Health Lodge for the start this historic royal tour of Camp Minwassin.

This photograph was signed and dated by HRH Prince Charles on the occasion of his visit to Camp Minwassin.   *Courtesy of* The Ottawa Citizen

In the meantime, campers hurried to various activity sites to be visited by the prince. These group activities included pioneering, rope bridge and rope climbing events, campfire and wilderness cooking demonstrations, an archery range competition, crafts, first aid activities, a visit with campers of the Voyageur Cabin, swimming, canoeing, and sailing.

A flotilla of small watercraft, bearing residents from around Mink Lake and surrounding communities, floated off the camp waterfront under the watchful eye of the OPP Marine Patrol. The prince acknowledged the cheers of these water-borne spectators, then turned his attention to the camp swimmers, canoeists, and sailing craft groups.

Upon leaving the waterfront, H.R.H. noticed a camper sitting alone on the equipment lodge steps, with white blotches of calamine lotion all over his body.

"Now, what do we have here?" Prince Charles asked, as he departed from his escort, and walked towards the boy.

"Poison ivy, sir," the executive director responded.

"Why is he over here?" the prince asked.

"To isolate him from other campers, sir."

Prince Charles wished the camper "A speedy recovery."

While the prince met with the wives of board members at the camp manager's cabin, all the campers, and the media representatives, assembled in the dining hall.

Upon the arrival of the official party, lunch was served. The use of stainless steel tableware, for only the head table, was the concession made to accommodate our royal visitor.

Menu
Hot dogs on buns
Potato chips
Carrot and celery sticks
Jell-O cream pudding
Fruit juice or milk
Tea or coffee for the visitors

Following the meal, Prince Charles talked to the campers about the need to protect the environment. He said that it was the duty of everyone to protect spring-fed waters, such as Mink Lake. That Canada and Canadians are blessed with a sound and healthy environment. That the beauty of the great out-of-doors of this land is the birthright of future generations of Canadians, and that those here today have the responsibility to see that it is nurtured, protected, and passed on for future generations to enjoy.

After lunch the prince was introduced to me; at that time I was the manager of the Centre Town Clubhouse. H.R.H. showed a keen interest in the Club's history; the guidance/counselling services; our outreach program to children and youth living in public housing complexes; to inner city/multi-problem families; and youngsters who may be in conflict with the law, family, and/or school. The prince expressed his personal thanks for making his camp visit so memorable.

A grand march of campers, with Prince Charles in their midst, made its way back to the baseball field while singing, "This Land is Your Land" and "The Happy Wanderer."

After bidding goodbye to his official party, and a final Eeeeeee . . . POW! cheer from our campers, H.R.H. strapped himself into the pilot's seat, put on a white helmet, and took off. Leaning out of the cockpit window the prince waved. Even though the downdraft from the helicopter had bowled some unsuspecting onlookers off their feet, many campers remained in their places until all three helicopters had departed, and the rat-tat-tat sound of their blades faded into the distance.

With the passing of the years a number of those 153 campers and staff who participated in this historic royal visit have stopped by the Club to recall a personal highlight or a royal encounter they had on this happy and historic occasion—clearly an experience that will live with them for many years to come.

Commentary:

A month following the royal visit, I sent to the Prince of Wales several photographs, with a brief note as a keepsake of his first visit to Canada. Shortly thereafter, an envelope arrived with the Buckingham Place coat of arms, and contained one of these photographs signed, "Charles 1970."

Governor General and Madame Roland Michener accept Christmas gifts made by Boys and Girls Club members.   *Author*

LETTERS FROM SUMMER CAMP

Camp Minwassin has since 1924 provided a camping experience that renews the body, expands the mind, and invigorates the spirit.

The thrill of catching one's first fish . . . racing before the wind in a sailboat . . . overnight camping under canvas . . . swimming and canoeing on spring-fed Mink Lake . . . developing outdoor survival skills . . . obtaining an appreciation of our natural environment . . . learning new sports . . . establishing friendships that last a lifetime . . . sharing the fellowship of a campfire that lifts the spirit and warms the heart . . . all of these and more have been offered to uncounted thousands of campers for eighty years.

The following are quotable quotes from "Letters from Summer Camp" received from children attending Camp Minwassin and published in the Fall 1988 edition of *Clubhouse News*.

This year I had fun at Camp Minwassin. My favourite activity was swimming. . . . They have good food.   *Billie Slaughter, age 14*

I have been going to Camp Minwassin for four years and each time I've enjoyed myself tremendously. The first year I went I was a little nervous, but it was OK and I had lots of fun. When my friends complain about nothing to do over the summer, I simply mention Camp Minwassin. I love that Camp.   *Angela Mills, age 11*

The thing I like about Camp is the Counsellor Mark Kurby, on exchange from Britain, because he was fun and easy going. Last year I did the Canadian Pioneer Council activity and loved it so much that I want to do it again this year. Next year I want to go up as a L.I.T. (a Leader in Training) so I can become a Camp Counsellor.

Paul Gordon, age 12

I had fun at Camp Minwassin; my favourite activity was "Kidnapped." My favourite Counsellor was Alain. My favourite Senior Staff was Patti. I hope to go back to Camp next year.

Kevin Webb, age 13

I had a great time at Camp and really liked my Cabin Counsellor. My favourite game was "Capture the Flag."   *Bobby Boileau, age 13*

I had a great time at Minwassin, it was the best Camp I ever went to. It was really neat when they had the "Mud Fight." I made a lot of friends. . . . I'm planning to go back next year.

Crystal Childs, age 11

Well, I liked so many things up at Camp Minwassin . . . the games . . . Counsellors . . . "Candlelight Ceremony" . . . it felt like home to me. As a L.I.T. (Leader in Training) I liked doing Kevin's job, saying all the announcements for the games . . . the best part was the "Mud Fight" and doing R.A.T. (night check) with the Counsellors. I would like to go back up as a Camp Counsellor next year so I could tell my kids about it when I grow up.   *Tina Pritchard, age 14, Leader in Training*

Commentary:

Feedback, be it positive or negative, provides valuable insights that institutional leaders and managers can use when evaluating goals, objectives and programs. It serves as a guide when future activities are adjusted or planned for the future.

BREATHE ON ME . . . IF YOU DARE!

Personal hygiene, or the lack of it, was a challenge that camp staff had to address each and every summer. This recurring problem was the subject of all pre-camp training sessions with Camp Minwassin counsellors.

To assist in getting the discussion underway, I invited former camp staff to share their problems related to personal hygiene with campers in previous years.

Jim began, "I have had a devil of a problem getting a couple of campers to keep their hair both clean and combed."

"The guys in my cabin last year were not too bad. My big problem was to get them to brush their teeth, at least once a day—or once a week!" Marc added.

"Ha. I had one boy who refused to shower. All I can say is thank God for the fact that he went for a swim a couple of times each camp session," Kevin shared.

"At least your guy went for a swim," Dale cut in. "In my cabin, last year, we had this guy who refused to shower or swim, never mind wash himself. Thank goodness for the nurse letting him shower in the health lodge. I think he would have returned home smelling very high," Dale added with a laugh.

"Eddie. Your campers were the older Woodmen's Cabin group, right?" I asked.

"That's right, Bernie," he replied.

"And do you have any insights to share with us?"

"Well, Bernie, campers seem to find creative excuses and ways for avoiding washing, showers, combing hair and brushing their teeth."

There was a buzz of agreement among his co-workers.

"But when they get to the age of the Woodsmen, they seem to be very conscious of their appearance. Last year my biggest difficulty was the great amount of time they spent grooming themselves!"

Walking over to the large pad on its easel, I said, "Let's list some imaginative ways we could use to improve camper hygiene this year."

Picking up the large felt marker pen I challenged, "Come on, call 'em out . . ."

"Group teeth brushing session!"

"Make it a rule that campers must swim at least once a week."

"Have everyone in a cabin take part in a water war or splash party in the shallow part of the swimming area of the lake."

"Ask the nurse or the senior staff to have a talk with campers who do not look after their personal hygiene—tell them it could make them and others sick."

"How about your 'breath test,' Bernie?" Gary asked.

"First of all, let's review some of your suggestions. When you compel campers to do things en masse, those who normally co-operate may perceive that they are being punished. This could lead to either camper rebellion against the cabin leader or retaliation on the one or two non-conformists," I explained, drawing a red line through point number one.

"Don't we have enough rules? Shall I cross it off?" I pointed to the second suggestion.

"Yeah . . ." "Sure thing . . ." "Too true!" were the mixed comments from the gathering.

I made a wide red streak across the sheet.

"This third one. How do you propose dealing with those campers who are afraid, if not terrified, of the water? Now, a water war in the showers, by campers in their swimsuits, sounds like fun. It just might be both fun *and* workable," Dale suggested.

"Way to go, Dale," someone exclaimed.

"Dale has touched on an approach that we know works. You have to understand that some youngsters may never have had to share a shower with anyone. So please be sensitive to their shyness or reluctance to shower with the group. The water war idea may help solve a quandary."

"What about the breath test, sir," a new counsellor asked, as he waved his hand in the air to get my attention.

"Yeah," was the response of several others.

"Well . . . er . . . I think the 'breathe on me' worked because of my position and the children's wish to gain my approval," I revealed.

"It really works," Marc cut in. "The counsellors look forward to it, during Bernie's weekend visits to camp," he explained to those around him.

"How does it work? What do you do?" asked Roger, a first-year counsellor.

"Are you sure you want to hear about this?" I inquire.

"Sure thing!" was the collective response.

"Well, back in 1970, on one of my first visits to camp, I was informed of this problem. The senior staff, Eric and Tom, notified me that no amount of talk, lectures, discussions or ultimatums would get some of their young charges to brush their teeth," I explained, as I placed the cap on the felt pen and then sat on the edge of a table.

"In an attempt to instill this good health habit, some of the counsellors established a routine that required all the cabin residents to show up at the washroom, toothbrushes in hand. It did not take the campers very long to find inventive ways to undercut or frustrate this group process. They resorted to fights, fake runaways, phony medical calls and downright disobedience."

I returned to my chair in the circle of camp staff.

"It caused a great deal of ill-will. That first year, I observed that campers were indifferent to the Sunday inspections. By the end of that season, I had volunteered to do the inspections, starting the next year."

"But what did you do?" was the frustrated whisper.

"On my first one or two inspections I was struck by the number of unwrapped bars of soap and unused tubes of toothpaste that lay in the camper's lockers. Another thing was the number of candy and food wrappers that campers threw on the tops of their lockers.

"I made it clear that it was the campers who were the object of these inspections. My intention was to overcome their apathetic attitudes by having the inspections focus on hands, fingernails, faces and ears. Those who were clean were released to play. The uncooperative campers had to try a second time to satisfy my high standards for their personal hygiene."

"But what about that breath test thing. How did that come about?" Roger pressed.

"Well, to keep a long story short, it must have been in the second or third inspection that it happened. It was a spur-of-the-moment thing. During an inspection of the Pioneer's Cabin, I think it was, I observed a partially used tube of Colgate toothpaste, with about three toothbrushes. On coming out of the cabin I asked for those who had cleaned their teeth to raise their hands. They all shot their hands skyward. In order to find out who really cleaned their teeth I walked up to the campers and challenged each one to "breathe on me if you dare!" Some thought it was a big joke and exhaled lungfuls of foul breath over me, between their giggles."

The camp counsellors chuckled.

"I then announced that Keith and Steve were the only campers who had cleaned their teeth. Furthermore, that they used Colgate. Keith and Steve were free to go and play while the others had to go to the washroom and brush their teeth. That was the start of it."

"Wow. How simple," someone exclaimed.

"When I went on to inspect the next cabin, some of the campers volunteered to have me smell their breath. You see, they had cleaned their teeth. I ignored them."

A ground swell of laughter arose from my listeners.

"So you see, only those fellows who had cleaned their teeth would volunteer to breathe on me. However, this self-incrimination was not to last very long. The message was received and understood by the campers. Someone said earlier, that campers could find creative ways to get around our rules and tests. I have to tell you that some campers found a way to get around my breath test. Would you like to know how they did it?"

"Sure," "You knew they did it?" "How did you know?" were some of their questions.

"Well, campers who were too lazy or too late to go to the washroom to clean their teeth, resorted to placing a little dab of toothpaste on their finger tip and then rubbing it over their teeth. So if I were to select them to breathe on me, the smell of fresh toothpaste would be unmistakable."

My audience was by now enjoying the story and the temerity of these youngsters.

"Ha guys, but I got them, for the most part. You see, by not rinsing out their mouths with water, the toothpaste coated the tongue, gums and the creases in the corner of the mouth. But I give them credit and a grudging respect for finding a way to circumvent the regulation. In fact I developed the ability to be able to tell the campers the brand of toothpaste they used."

I became aware the camp staff had broken into applause.

"Thanks, guys. I knew that we had won the battle for personal hygiene when the campers started to mix different brands of toothpaste, in an attempt to confuse my sense of smell."

"Smart kids!" someone remarked.

"While all this toothpaste stuff was going on we instituted hygiene standards for beds, stored clothing, lockers, floors, grounds, and the rafters of each cabin.

"In conclusion, I would invite a camper to assist me with the inspection. I would take that opportunity to discuss the standards and benefits of keeping bedding free of sand, to prevent rashes; removing damp clothing that could smell and/or become unusable; moving suitcases and storage bags to ensure that the floor under them had been swept; in particular, disposing of scraps of food and wrappers, as they could attract vermin; checking the tops of lockers and the rafters for contraband and refuse; paying attention to personal hygiene; and improving the general appearance of each cabin.

"Once the inspection was completed, the cabin representative would report our findings to his cabin mates. A second youngster would be selected for the grounds inspection, followed by a brief report to the campers.

"One final point. Each one of you must discover what leadership style works best for you. The challenge is for you to find a way of involving or winning over the youngsters, so that they work with you. I know how to do it, given my size, voice and position. By sharing with you some insights as to how I think and react in my leadership role, there may be an idea or suggestion you will want to include in your particular style of leadership this year."

The staff training workshop adjourned for lunch.

Commentary:

- Leaders must refrain from the temptation to discipline the whole group for the transgressions of a few or an unknown individual.
- Leaders who deal with children and youth even-handedly win their respect, co-operation and loyalty.
- Leaders who challenge those they lead to participate in finding resolutions to problems ensure the growth and confidence of both parties.

- Leaders should acquire the skills to neutralize those individuals who use the group situation to disguise their antisocial behaviour. It is a technique that has to be constantly honed.
- Leaders with experience in group dynamics can nullify the negative influence of a potential troublemaker.
- Leaders need to develop inventive techniques to solve recurring problems.
- By not being too predictable in their verbal rejoinders, leaders keep their charges off balance and receptive to the benefits of a positive relationship.

CAMPERS' REVOLT

There was an unexpected reaction to my going to camp "winged"—that is, with a broken leg.

The light-hearted mocking that was carried out and countered before the assembled campers, following dinner on Saturday, had an interesting effect and unexpected repercussions.

You should keep in mind that it happened during my first visit to Camp Minwassin, following the breaking of my right leg.

From the moment I arrived, the campers showed great concern about me. They fussed over me, sought to fetch me chairs, offered to carry my briefcase, and so on. They shared with me regrets that I would not be able to lead a game of "Simon Says" or participate in the mud fight and other activities.

The children had me tell the story of how I broke my leg, over and over again. It seemed to amaze and amuse them, that a grown adult could be the victim of such a freak accident. The campers' empathy and the staff's bemused attitude to my predicament would eventually lead to a surprising turn of events.

I would call it a "campers' revolt."

It all started with the after-dinner announcements on Saturday.

Kevin, who had attended Camp Minwassin as a camper, leader in training, counsellor and waterfront director, was officer of the day and scheduled to make the daily after-dinner announcements.

Over the years, Kevin and I had grown to know and trust each other. The two of us shared a similar sense of humour and felt free to rib each other. Consequently, he took every opportunity to make light of me, whether it was my style of dress, my English accent, the knee-high socks, or whatever.

Kevin's exploits went as far as assigning a junior camp staff member to cut off my tie, whenever I wore one, at camp. So popular was this antic, that it became an annual ritual. Consequently, I played my part in this prank to the hilt, much to the chagrin of the unfortunate first-year junior counsellor who had been assigned to cut my tie.

Throughout the years there grew an abiding mutual respect and appreciation between us.

So it was that Kevin, with his tongue firmly planted in his cheek, delivered a humorous monologue to the camp population. He was in fine form, as he attempted to explain how I broke my leg, with a series of smart remarks and jokes.

The din from 100 campers and forty-three staff in noisy response drowned out some of his delicious humour. Kevin acted out each and every line. It was a performance that would be the envy of most actors.

My attention was drawn to the reaction of the audience. It was clearly divided.

The camp staff, leaders in training and older campers had a rollicking reaction. The first-time campers, particularly the younger ones, were somewhat puzzled. They joined with the intermediate campers, as they hissed, booed, and heckled Kevin's every comment.

Campers in the east end of the dining hall, where I was sitting, expressed their sympathy. They patted me on the shoulder; some asked that I not get upset; others thumped the table top in an effort to drown out the speaker.

Finally, Kevin had finished. He held me with a mischievous gleam in his eyes. It was clear that he was issuing a challenge for me to match his performance.

Raising my hand I requested and received permission to address the camp population. When I arose from my chair and hobbled to the centre of the dining hall, the majority of the campers let out a loud and sustained cheer.

As I stood in the centre of this cavernous building, I fixed my eyes on Kevin. He had taken his seat at the senior staff table, to my right. We winked at each other. He tried to quiet the campers so I could speak. But the children's response was to renew their cheering in support of me. They would have nothing to do with him, for now.

Calm returned to the assembly. I felt that the conflicting responses I had observed between the campers and staff could be exploited. It also provided me with an opportunity to turn the situation to my advantage.

"Thank you, Kevin—"

Boos cut me off. I raised my hand and obtained order immediately.

"As I was saying. Thank you, Kevin, for reminding the campers and me about the dangers of housework," I said, in a soft voice that forced my listeners to pay attention.

"You're welcome," was Kevin's response. The senior staff chuckled their approval.

"Campers," I began, "given the real dangers inherent in housekeeping that Kevin has properly pointed out to all of us, and of which I am living proof, it is necessary that we take immediate action to ensure the safety of each and every one of you."

"What's he up to?" the assistant camp manager asked Kevin, in a hoarse whisper, from their nearby table.

"You'll see," I shot back.

"Effective immediately, from this day onwards, only the camp staff will clean the cabins and the grounds," I shouted, so that one and all could hear me.

The moans and groans of the camp staff were quickly drowned out as the dining hall exploded with cheers. The roll of thunder from 100 pairs of hands banging on the tabletops, and the rumble of hundreds of little feet stomping on the floor indicated the delight and approval of the campers. The children sustained this thunderous noise level for several minutes, in spite of the efforts of all the counsellors to stop it.

Senior staff sat as if riveted to their chairs. All remained unsmiling. Kevin's chin dropped. Then a wink lit up his flushed face with a great big smile. He had tuned into what I was doing.

It took several minutes to restore order.

Once calm had been restored, I said, "Now remember, campers, only counsellors are responsible for cleaning your cabins. We don't wish to have any of you campers injured doing housework . . . DO WE?" I cupped a hand to my ear, to encourage their response.

"NO!" yelled the campers in reply.

The thunder of their pounding hands and feet rolled once more, up and down the length of the dining hall, from table to table.

"I think we owe Kevin a big hand for bringing these dangers to our attention. Thank you, Kevin," I said, mockingly.

A large number of the campers waved one hand in the air in Camp Minwassin's version of "giving someone a big hand." I resumed my seat among the campers.

The assistant camp manager made several routine announcements regarding the evening's activities before she dismissed the group.

As the campers dispersed to their cabins, it became apparent from their comments that they were delighted with the directive I had handed down, in my capacity as the CEO of Camp Minwassin. They exchanged high fives, pats, and hugs with me as they exited the dining hall. They relished the discomfort of the staff.

I felt very pleased with myself, in that I had been able to turn the joke back on Kevin and the staff. However, it turned out to be a joke that was to have an unexpected impact.

The following morning was bright and sunny. I set up a worktable outside the kitchen. I must have been there for over an hour and a half, going through the ever-present paperwork. This day it included a review of the midyear report of the three clubhouses in the city; and the schedule of the Clubhouse Special Events Calendar, for the approaching fall season, had to be finalized.

The assistant camp manager stopped by to plead, "Can you do something about the camper revolt?"

"What camper revolt? What is this, another one of Kevin's jokes?" I countered, rather nonchalantly.

"It's no joke, Bernie. The campers refuse to clean up their cabins, make their bunk beds, or clean the grounds. Come on, you started it all, with that declaration of yours, after dinner last night. It is almost time for Sunday inspection and I am told that the cabins are a hell of a mess," she explained sombrely.

It was clear that this was a serious problem. Consequently, I started to place the unfinished paperwork in my briefcase.

"When I asked why they will not clean up their cabins, their response is simply, 'Bernie said.' I think it is time you told the campers that you were only clowning around," she added.

I chuckled to myself, as I headed towards my quarters, in the Health Lodge.

"Jerred. Come here, please," I called to a camper, as he left the Health Lodge. "Would you please inform the campers that I will be doing the Sunday inspection. I expect to get there in about half an hour. Okay?"

"But Bernie, I don't think any of the cabins are ready," the boy spluttered.

"Why on earth would that be?" I demanded.

"Because of what you said in the dining hall. You know, last night," he explained, wide-eyed.

"But my young friend, that was a joke. We all had a good laugh at Kevin's expense. He was joking with me, so I made one in return. Now it seems that the campers have made the joke backfire on me."

There was an ear-to-ear smile on the face of the boy in front of me. "I'll tell 'em!" Jerred said.

"What I want you to tell them is that I will be over there to do the inspection in about half an hour. Go on, get out of here!" I playfully swung my crutch in his direction.

"Hey, guys! Bernie is doing the inspection. Bernie is coming!"

The boy yelled at the top of his voice, as he ran as fast as his feet could carry him into the boys' section.

A few moments later several campers appeared on the path that led to the boys' section. "Bernie, is it true?" one of the boys yelled.

"Is what true?" I asked.

"That you will do the inspection today?" he quizzed.

"Sure is," I replied, as I placed the crutches under each arm and stumbled in their direction.

The campers vanished into the bushes and trees that screened the boy's section. "Bernie's coming . . . There's an inspection . . ." calls drifted on the wind.

I envisioned the rush and hubbub that the phrase "Bernie's coming" was causing among the campers.

I allowed sufficient time to elapse as I lingered at the arts and crafts cabin. Another "rest" at the basketball court, which was in full view of the boys' section. I observed that campers scurried about in anticipation of a tough inspection. Their equipment, cabin and grounds were soon in order.

Upon arriving in the boys' section I found campers standing in straight lines outside their respective cabins.

"Inspection will be done, but not by me after all. My leg hurts too much. I will have the youngest camper in each cabin do the inspection today."

The children greeted this with enthusiasm. As they inspected the inside of each cabin, I took to checking the hands, faces, knees and breath of the line of campers.

"I want to thank all of you for making my joke against Kevin and the camp staff so effective. But now the joke is over and it is back to the regular routine. Thank you. Have a good day."

There was an audible groan from the campers. As for myself, I felt that I had betrayed the campers. But it was necessary to have order restored once again, by me.

Commentary:

- The fact that the campers could get their cabins and grounds in good order in such a short period of time was testimony to the co-operative relationship that existed between the campers and their counsellors.
- It also underscored their sense of pride, their high standards, and the folklore of Camp Minwassin, which dates back six decades.
- Youngsters can use such situations to test and expand their relationship with their peers, their leaders and, most importantly, themselves.

THE CAMP MIMIC

Knee-high socks; oversize white running shoes; tennis shorts; short-sleeved shirt; a necktie; an over-expanded waistline; a wide leather belt; and a set of oversized glasses perched on his nose. These were the props used by sixteen-year-old Damian, a Camp Minwassin counsellor, to mimic me.

Damian had chosen to stroll from building to building in such a way that he would be shielded from my field of vision. However, he was in the full view of the thirty-five campers and six staff who were attending the Special Events workshop that I was leading.

The following is my recollection of what happened.

Shortly after the Special Events workshop began, I noticed that all the heads of the campers and staff moved from left to right in unison. Out of curiosity, I stole a glance over my right shoulder. There was nothing to be seen.

Regaining the camper's attention, I returned to the subject at hand. All seemed to be going well until I realized that all heads were now moving from right to left.

Clearing my throat loudly, I sought to retain the attention of my young charges.

Grins, smiles, and bemused expressions were on the faces of all of the campers, with the exception of eight-year-old Robbie. He looked around at his fellow campers, then back to the area behind me, with a puzzled expression on his little face.

I made another slow turn in an effort to discover what was so amusing, only to find nothing. Returning my attention to the youngsters, I observed that Robbie had raised his hand skyward, ready to ask a question. After bringing the bemused group back to some sense of normality, I turned to the young camper.

"Yes Robbie, what is it?" I asked.

"Well, it's Damian. He looks just like you, Bernie," he said innocently.

This led to hoots, yells, laughter and cheers from the group. It lasted several minutes. Now realizing that I was the butt of a well-planned joke, I knew that I had to be careful not to over-react.

As the group settled down of its own accord, I called at the top of my voice for Damian to show himself. There was a moment of absolute silence. Even the birds seemed to stop singing. Then Damian stepped out from behind the Tuck Shop. I carefully looked over my teenage mimic.

"Robbie, I don't think Damian looks like me. You see, I don't wear white running shoes, and what's more my tummy is not that big."

The campers drowned out the remainder of my critique as they collapsed in another round of howls and shrieks of good-natured laughter. They leapt out of their places and took great delight in pointing out how well the mimic had replicated his subject, to the enjoyment of one and all.

The only two who held their original seated positions were Robbie and I. We made eye contact, which we held as calm returned to the group that surrounded us.

Raising his hand once more, Robbie slowly looked over his fellow campers, and with tears in his eyes, asked. "What did I say? Why are they all laughing at me?" he pouted.

With that, I too joined in this chorus of laughter. Reaching over to Robbie, I gave the little boy a hug. "It's Damian and me they are all laughing at—not you, Robbie," I reassured this first-year camper.

"Oh!" he exclaimed, and joined the campers in cheering Damian.

Campers broke ranks and mobbed Damian. They patted his oversized tummy.

"Hey, Damian. I lost twenty pounds this year," I shouted above the noise of the crowd.

A broad smile and the thumbs-up sign bridged the space between the mimic and the butt of the joke.

A somewhat reserved individual, Damian became a hero to many campers. Another thread was added to the folklore of Camp Minwassin that dates back to 1924.

Commentary:

- Youngsters get an extra delight out of "putting one over" on a leader.
- A leader's willingness to participate in such good-natured activities develops the bonds of trust and loyalty that can be to the mutual benefit of all.
- Too many leaders tend to envision themselves above the good-natured ribbing or interaction of those they seek to lead.
- Youngsters tend to use such occasions to expand their comfort level with, and to obtain an insight into, their leader's reaction to new situations.
- Such interaction and acceptance between generations are the building blocks of trust, which can be used and tested with time.
- Today, Damian works as an activity leader for the YMCA.

THE BUTTERFLY WING

It was a hot July day. Lunch had just finished and the campers were scheduled to have their daily rest period in their cabins.

All the windows and doors of the Bushman Cabin were open to catch and benefit from a very light breeze, which did nothing to cool off the interior of the cabin. Consequently, the counsellor of the youngest boys in Camp Minwassin had the good judgment to allow his young charges to enjoy the rest period in the shade of nearby trees and bushes.

Released from the confines of their cabin, these first-time campers quietly explored the bush and ground cover about them.

"Bernie, are you busy right now?" Mark, the junior counsellor of the Bushman Cabin asked, as I made my way to the camp office.

"I have a scheduled meeting with the camp manager. Why do you ask, Mark?" I responded.

"The counsellor has had to take Roger to the nurse and I have to get the "tuck order" for my cabin. I'm not allowed to leave the campers unattended. Could you stay with them for a few minutes?" Mark asked, as he looked over his young charges. "I won't be too long," he added.

"Okay. But stop by the camp office and tell Rick that I will be late. And that I am covering your cabin," I countered.

"Sure will." He turned to the campers. "Hey, you guys co-operate with Bernie while I go and get your tuck," he said, before going to pick up their midday treat.

Over the years, our campers have accepted the rest period as a part of their daily routine. They read comics, play cards, plan campfire skits, write letters home, and talk quietly among themselves.

Settling into the shade, I took this opportunity to relax. But unfortunately it was not for long.

"Bernie. Randy is in the bushes. He's got something in his hand," whispered Carl, the youngest boy in camp.

Having dozed off, I became fully alert as Carl tapped my forearm. "Look, look, over there, Bernie. Randy has something in his hand," Carl repeated with a slight shrill in his voice.

Five interested campers started to move in Randy's direction.

They halted in their tracks with my suggestion, "Let Randy bring whatever he has over to us. In the meantime we should all stay still so that whatever he has in his hand will not become frightened."

Tim took the first look at what was in Randy's hand.

"Oh. It's a butterfly!" he exclaimed.

"All right guys, no crowding. Let's all sit down. That way we can all get a good look at Randy's butterfly," I advised.

When Randy arrived in the middle of the group he removed the cupped hand that had served as a wind guard. He revealed a large yellow and black butterfly perched on his index finger.

"Let it go! Let it go," was the immediate response of several of the Bushmen.

Throughout the excitement Carl remained silent. He moved so that he stood behind me, as I sat on the ground.

"Its wing is broken," Randy said softly.

"Let me see," I asked.

"Randy, I can't see any break," was my first reaction.

"You can see it when the butterfly opens its wings. He won't open them now," Randy explained, with a tinge of frustration in his voice.

"Blow very gently on the butterfly from behind," I advised.

Lifting the insect to his lips, Randy gave a soft puff of air from behind. The insect unfolded its wings. It showed clearly that the right wing was severed almost in half.

"Oh!" "Ahhh!" "It's nice," were the gasps and responses to the colour and design on the wings of this beautiful insect.

"What do we do now?" asked Stan.

"Put it back on a branch of a bush where Randy found it. Let Mother Nature take care of things," was my suggestion.

"Can't we fix it?" Stan inquired.

"No, I don't think so," Randy advised, as he stood up.

By now little Carl had placed both of his hands on the top of my head. He was resting his chin on his hands.

"Take it to the nurse," Carl said, in a clear voice, for all to hear.

The whole cabin group looked in his direction.

"What did you say, Carl?" Randy asked, one hand protecting his eyes from the bright sun.

"Take it to the nurse. She can fix it," Carl asserted, as he moved from behind me.

The other boys let out a spontaneous laugh at this suggestion.

"No she can't," Randy stated indignantly.

"Yes she can!" Carl shouted, as he stepped forward and stood to my left.

"The nurse has those butterfly Band-Aids. I've seen them," the little boy announced, as he turned towards me for assurance.

Smiles swept across the faces of every one.

"That's a good idea, Carl," I cut in before anyone could make a smart remark that might hurt this considerate young camper. "But I think those Band-Aids would be too heavy and would prevent the butterfly from flying away."

"Oh. I see," said Carl sadly.

Randy returned the butterfly to the bushes.

"Okay. Who ordered the chips . . . the Smarties . . . ?" It was Mark with their Tuck Shop order.

So it was, that Randy placed the butterfly back in the bush and I went about my business.

Following the rest period the residents of the Bushman Cabin embarked on a nature hike with their counsellors. Their reaction and concern for the butterfly led me to believe that at this early age, these boys have an appreciation for wild life, the ecology, and the environment. That is an insight our Camp Minwassin has been providing to inner city children and youth since it began.

Commentary:

- When H.R.H. The Prince of Wales made his first official visit to Canada and Camp Minwassin in July 1970, he informed the young campers of their individual and collective duty to become actively involved in the protection of the environment. Prince Charles stressed that it was the responsibility of each and every one to protect the lakes, trees, wild life, and the unspoiled out-of-doors that is the natural heritage of Canada.

- Camp Minwassin has striven to provide inner city children and youth with the opportunity to experience, appreciate and benefit from the natural wilderness setting that is their birthright.

EPILOGUE

Thank You for Remembering

In the first six to nine months after assuming the position as director of the Centre Town Clubhouse of the Ottawa Boys Club (now the Boys and Girls Club of Ottawa), I found my method of work, and every action, being compared to those of Fred C. McCann, who began the Club in 1923.

Comments such as: "In Mr. McCann's day that would not happen . . ." "If Fred saw that he would turn over in his grave . . ." "When Fred was here we did things this way . . . [or that way]" "Mr. McCann would never allow that . . ." Such comments are an understandable reaction to the loss of the gentle, familiar, predictable, but firm, leadership of a much-beloved man.

I'm confident that had Fred McCann been around during such encounters, he would have said, "Thanks for remembering—but this is a new day and a new leadership style."

Rather than trying to be a carbon copy of the founder by attempting to emulate his style, I viewed these constant comparisons as a challenge. They enabled me to grow, develop my own leadership style, and introduce new programs, while remaining true to my own character and personality.

As the months passed from the spring, through the summer, and into the fall program seasons of that first year, such comparisons lessened. The moment of truth that confirmed acceptance of my leadership style came in November of that first year. Following a board of directors meeting I escorted Thomas G. Lowrey and Emmanuel Glatt, both founding board members in 1923, and past presidents of the Club, to the front door.

A commotion broke out among several Club members in the lobby. I had to excuse myself to restore calm and order among the boys.

Upon returning to these gentlemen, who had observed my actions, Mr. Glatt commented to his companion: "Just like Fred McCann!"

There followed more than twenty years of great personal and professional satisfaction in working with the volunteer and professional staff of the Club and the Ottawa community. Together we saw the Club grow from approximately 800 boys in one facility and summer camp to over 4,600 boys and girls in three, full-service, dynamic clubhouses and year-round camps.

Such spectacular accomplishments could only have been made possible by the firm foundation laid down by Fred C. McCann, and the wellspring of goodwill that has resulted from many years of meaningful service provided by our Boys and Girls Club.

For many boys and girls, plus myself, "The Club" was truly a home away from home.

Eventually I retired. This provided the opportunity to have surgery on my left eye. Furthermore, it marked the end of a fifty-two-year separation from my family, due to World War II, with whom I have become joyfully reunited.

To avoid those who would come after me from suffering the constant comparisons I endured in my early years with the Club, I resolved to participate in only those Club functions to which I received a specific invitation. This would mean that from time to time I would have to be satisfied with enjoying organizational accomplishments, and historic milestones, vicariously from a discreet distance.

Nevertheless, in the years since I retired, my spirits continue to be lifted when former Club members approach to recall some kindness, some difficulty, some ability, some special event, or of a friendship made that had lasted a lifetime, in which the Club—or I—had played a key role during their formative years.

Their touching comments are a validation of my lifetime of service. I count myself to be most fortunate to have learned first-hand that I may have made some small difference for good in the lives of so many boys and girls during their formative years.

On such occasions I say: "Thank you for remembering . . . it's important!"

It has been estimated that well over 250,000 youngsters, from six to eighteen years of age, have benefited from their membership in the Boys and Girls Club of Ottawa, since it was founded in 1923.

Bernard J. Muzeen, P. Mgr.
Author

RECORD OF CHILDREN AND YOUTH SERVICES

11th Oshawa Scout Troop .... Assistant Leader *
Oshawa Boys Club .... Program Supervisor
Legislative Select Committee on Youth .... Resource Person *
Victoria Park Project, Calgary .... Community Worker *
Company of Young Canadians........................ Operations Officer
Ottawa Boys Club .... Group Club Leader *
Boys and Girls Club of Ottawa–Carleton .... Executive Director
OUR KIDS & National Child Day .... Co-Founder *
Canadian Mothercraft.................................... Development Officer
City of Kanata—Youth Recreation.................. Activity Leader *
Bereaved Families .... Development Officer
"Fair Prices at the Pump" Coalition................ Spokesman *
Aboriginal Sacred Assembly .... Project Coordinator
Skateboard for Youth in Stittsville.................. Instructor *
Kanata Youth Centre..................................... Dance Chaperon *

*Volunteer Position